SHAUNTA KENERLY
AMB PUBLISHING

Copyright© 2014 By Shaunta Kenerly

ISBN-13: **978-0692338100**
ISBN-10: **0692338101**

PUBLISHED BY: AMB PUBLISHING

COVER ART: AMB BRANDING DESIGN

COVER MODELS: AMBER PARIS, BEANNA DAVISON, & male model BOZ

PHOTOGRAPHER: SHANGHAI IMAGING

EDITED BY: NICOLE SCOTT

To order additional copies of this book, contact:

Shaunta Kenerly

Follow me on Twitter @shaunkenerly

shauntakenerly@yahoo.com

follow the book & myself on facebook

SHAUNTA KENERLY
AMB PUBLISHING

Dedication

I dedicate this book to everyone who has lost their life to the streets. I also want to dedicate this book to all of the hustlers putting their life on the line every day to make money out there. Just know that every hustler has a chance to stop.

SHAUNTA KENERLY
AMB PUBLISHING

I0190321

ESCAPING THE ALLURE OF THE GAME

"The game ain't over"

CHAPTER 1

Reese

It's been two years since the day Diana pushed me out of these front doors after being shot multiple times by Simone. I was hospitalized for a week. One bullet hit me in the shoulder and the other hit me near my spine. After surgery I had lost some feeling in my legs and feet. I have been coming here ever since for physical therapy.

My therapist has me in here three times a week for two hours per visit. I am glad to say that today will be my last visit. The doctors said that I have made a rapid recovery and I give God all of the glory.

I have been jogging for the last few months and doing some calisthenics to get my body back in shape. Diana is loving the new body. But I am constantly reminded by my scars. Some days when I am out in the hood, I find myself looking over my back as if I am still in the game. I wonder if Simone would be after me if she knew I was still alive. I wanted my revenge but Diana and

the smile on my son's face keeps me grounded.

Leaving the physical therapist office, I drive through the hood remembering the good ole days. Now some of the young dealers have come up and making themselves some money. A lot of them still salute me and talk about how our team use to run the streets. They also try to ask for my connect but I remind them that I am out and I will stay out. It's crazy how the game goes on even when someone gets locked up or killed.

Opening the door to my home, my son runs over to me as if he hasn't seen me all day. Diana laughs at us playing and acting silly with each other.

"How about we take a ride to the park today? It's so pretty out and your son has been begging me to take him," Diana asks putting on some gym shoes.

"Yeah, we can do that," I respond.

"Yeah!" Rico cheered.

We pull into the park parking-lot and all I can see are nice whips. I know that most of these rides are dope boy cars from the plush interior and wet paint jobs.

Diana and I walk Rico towards the playground and I hear someone shout my name. I pretend like I don't hear it but Diana makes sure that I did.

"Who's calling you?" she questions looking behind us.

"I don't know."

"Reese hold up!" Tone shouts running from the basketball court.

"What's up man," I say shaking his hand.

"Shit where you been? I tried calling you the other day," Tone replies looking me up and down.

"You already know. I've been cooling at the crib. Trying to stay out of the way you know," I casually reply.

"I can dig it. How's your back?" Tone asks.

"It's alright. I feel a little pain from time to time but besides that I am cool."

"Reese, little man and I will be over here," Diana interjects pointing at the playground.

"Okay babe."

"Man I need you to make that call to J for me," Tone says sounding desperate.

"Have you talked to Christian?" I ask waiting for a response.

"Man Christian is doing his own thing. We rarely see him. He is always on that damn highway making moves," Tone replies.

"B told me that they went down to see J last weekend," I say frowning up my face confused.

"Yeah, they did but that shit was gone before Monday morning."

"Damn y'all got rid of it that fast?" I ask amazed.

"Reese the shit is rolling. I mean the streets are so fucked up that we are the main crew putting people on. We just now have our own people. So when we sell out we are waiting for Christian again and he might be out of town." Tone says looking around making sure nobody is listening.

"Shit, I don't know what to tell you. All I can say is get with him. I can't tell him what to do."

"I understand that but we are losing money out here because he only fuck with us when he want to," Tone aggressively respond.

"I will talk to him but I can't make any promises," I say shaking his hand again.

"Bet."

Tone drives off in his new Mercedes Benz. I check out the car like I want to buy it. Shit I can't afford it now working on my fixed income.

Luckily I had to meet an old white man that wanted to sell his Laundromat. The Laundromat was doing well when he had it, he just wanted to retire. I made him a cash offer and he accepted it. The Laundromat continues to make me a profit but I do miss the easy money I use to make. I can only imagine how much money my boys are making.

After Tone leaves, I rush over to my family. I sneak on the play-set and surprise Rico running across the bridge. He falls down with laughter.

We spend about an hour playing with Rico until he fell asleep. Now it's momma and daddy time.

Diana and I share turns pushing Rico in his stroller along the wooded area. She really wants to get married now that I am feeling better. In fact, she has ideas for her dress, the venue, and color arrangements. I wasn't surprised. I didn't know how to tell her that I couldn't afford to pay for her dream wedding.

"Are you listening to me Reese?" Diana says with an attitude.

"Yes I am listening. I want to marry you. I do. But…"

Diana cuts me off, "But what?"

"We can't afford all the things you want," I say aggressively.

"Well you don't have to worry about that. My dad said that he will pay for everything but our honeymoon," Diana says with excitement.

"Really!" I shout stopping in my tracks.

"Yes. He is excited for us."

"That's wonderful. Well what do you want me to do?" I ask.

"I am planning a dinner at The Roof Top. I want you to make sure that your groomsmen attend," Diana answers.

"I never thought of who I wanted to be my groomsmen," I utter.

"Well you should be," Diana counters smacking her lips.

"I guess all of my boys."

"Who will be your best man? B or Christian?" she asks waiting for my response.

"I guess Christian. He's my brother so I guess that's what I should do."

"Okay well make sure he comes to dinner tomorrow," Diana instructs starring me in my eyes.

Diana and I push Rico for another 30 minutes or so until the sun started to set.

During the ride home, I just thought about making sure that everything will go perfectly for our wedding. The first thing I had to do was make sure that Christian would be able to be in the wedding. He always claims that he is busy. I never would have wished this hustler's life on him in a million years. But this is the road he chose.

I drop the family off and ride off to the Laundromat. My manager needs me to take the money to the bank. I don't trust anybody with my money except for Diana.

Arriving at the Laundromat, the manager waves me to follow him into the office. He counts out the money and I throw it in a Gucci bag. I give him his pay check and step out. He wants to show me two washing machines that has been acting up so I follow him again.

He is talking to me about the maintenance needed to fix the washers. I am listening but this thick ass brown skinned woman catches my eye. I couldn't help but stare at her luscious curves. She is only a few feet from us but her ass feels so close. She is bent over taking clothes out of the bottom dryer. Her shorts reveals her ass cheeks. Not too much but enough for my imagination. My eyes scroll up her body like a Xerox machine. Her plumped breasts are the most eye catching. Wearing a tank top I can see right through the shirt. She's showing her nipples and pierced bellybutton. I lick my lips as if I can taste her.

"She's bad ain't she? The manager whispers.

"Yes she's nice," I respond back but keeping my eyes on her.

"She always be taking selfies of herself. I believe she might be a model."

"Why do you say that?" I giggle.

"She poses all over the place. She sits up on the washing machines taking pics on her phone. She takes pics with the laundry carts. She even pose with her laundry detergent like she's working for a commercial ad," he says.

"She sure is fine enough to be a model," I respond.

"The first time she came in here she was asking about you?"

"About me?" I question.

"Yes. She wanted to know who owned the place," he states.

"How long ago was this?" I ask switching my attention to him.

"About a month ago," he answers quickly.

"Okay," I nod my head.

"Her name is Candace. She's in here every Sunday evening. I believe she stays in the apartments around the corner," the manager confesses.

"Oh yeah," I smile.

Trying to attempt to put her clothes basket on the folding table she almost fall. I rush to her aid and catch the basket.

"Thank you. I almost busted my ass," she admits laughing.

"No problem. I couldn't have you hurting yourself in here," I reply solemnly.

"That's nice of you."

"Thank you. I can't afford a lawsuit honestly," I say laughing.

"Aw, so you are the owner?" she questions but looking at Dennis the manager.

"Yes. I have been the owner for a while now."

"He told me he owned the place. I knew he was lying," she counters.

"So what's your name?" I ask.

"Candace," she smiles shaking my hand.

"My name is Reese," I say sitting her basket down on the table.

"Well Reese, can I call you some time? I believe I owe you for saving me," she questions pulling her cell phone from her back pocket.

"You don't owe me anything. How about I take your number and call you so you can have my number?"

"That will be fine," she blushed.

I helped her load her car, and we talked for another moment before I rolled out.

After making the bank deposit, I called Christian. I asked him to meet me at my house, but he insisted that I meet him at his spot. Normally, I would not meet anyone at a trap spot now that I am out of the game but I am doing it for Diana.

When I pull up to Christian's spot in the near-bye city of Springfield, he comes out with duffle bags in his hands. He tosses the bags in his trunk. After closing the trunk, he makes is way over to me.

"Let's take a ride brah," Christian instructs walking up to my driver's door.

"Ride where?" I question looking at him crazy.

"C'mon, I have a surprise for you," he says laughing walking back to his car.

"Man I don't like surprises, and you know I ain't fucking around with the bullshit," I spat aggressively.

"Reese I want even put you in that situation," Christian shook his head annoyed.

"So what's in the bag?"

"Don't worry about that, but to ease your mind, it ain't dope," Christian replied.

"Where are we going?" I pressed.

"We are going to take a ride over to Keith's."

"Why Keith's?" I wonder. I climb out of my truck and walk over to his car.

"That's the surprise," Christian says closing the door.

"Christian, I am going to follow you. I have something to do later."

We meet Keith at his crib and he seems happy to see me. I am now more curious to find out this surprise more than ever.

Keith sits us down and brings out a bottle of Patron with shot glasses. He fills all three glasses and we down them.

"I haven't told him yet Keith," Christian blurts out.

"Reese, I have some good news for you," Keith says.

"What is it?" I question with concern.

"I found where those girls are at."

"Yeah!" Christian cheers after taking another shot.

"What girls?" I question knowingly.

"Reese, he found the bitch that shot you!" Christian shouts.

"Calm down family," Keith interjects.

"Damn did you?" I say softly as my mind registers what he just said.

"Reese we can go get the bitches right now!" Christian says with excitement.

"Where are they?" I question.

"They are in Louisville," Keith answers taking a shot.

"Oh yeah," I say rubbing my hands together deep in thought.

"My people have been watching them. He said they came off like they were too good to be true and they described them to me. That's when I knew who it was. He wanted to get them then but he owes me a favor. Here check out these pics he sent me."

"Damn I don't know what to say. I had dreamed of finding her and each time I killed her different ways. I don't know what to say," I confess drinking straight from the bottle.

"I understand," Keith replies.

"Damn they are in Louisville?"

"Yup," Keith answers.

"They are right down the highway man. We can go down there for the weekend and kill each one of those scandalous bitches," Christian stresses.

"I have to think about it man," I say trying to switch gears.

"What is it to think about? I have already told Lamar about it and he's ready. I have a trunk full of shit for their ass!" Christian shouts getting in my face.

"Man, I just have a family now to think about," I say sternly.

"I just wanted to let you know. I know I would feel bad if I didn't let you know," Keith adds.

"Thanks. I appreciate that. I have to get ready for this wedding and all. It's just not in me anymore."

"Man fuck that! These bitches killed White Boy! Almost killed you and tortured your woman! If you don't do something about it I will!" Christian shouts.

"Christian if your brother put that behind him than you should respect that," Keith says calmly.

"I will do anything for my brother man!" Christian shouts causing tears to fill his eyes.

"Man if you want to do something for me, then I want you to be my best man at the wedding," I say grabbing Christian.

"Real shit?" Christian asks.

"Yeah man. That's starting with this dinner Diana has planned for tomorrow," I say hugging my brother.

"Do I have to pay," Christian asks jokingly.

"No man."

"I'm still going to get those bitches," Christian says pulling away.

CHAPTER 2

REESE

After leaving Keith's house, I decide to go to a new spot B and Tone had on the eastside of Dayton. I get off on Smithville Road and turn on a side street where the spot is. I ride around the block twice making sure that the spot wasn't being watched. Last thing I want is to get caught up in some shit that I'm no longer involved with.

The neighborhood predominantly is filled with white residents. I wonder how they are keeping a low profile riding in this neighborhood in nice cars and black as hell. I hope this was just a spot to work out of for a month or two then bounce to another. I park about four houses down from the spot. I felt weird walking into anybody's spot without my pistol. I now keep my pistol tucked away out of Rico's reach.

Approaching the house, I am nervous as hell. I haven't been in a spot in a while. Feel as if this is my first time going into one. From the sidewalk, I notice three cameras on the worn down house. Knowing B there's more cameras around back and even inside.

Jumping on the porch, I notice that their blinds are all cracked and bent from what I believe them constantly looking out. I bang on the door twice before the door slowly opens. My senses are heightened by the strong aroma of cooked cocaine. The smell will never leave my memory from all of the dope we have cooked up over the years.

"Come in and shut the door behind you!" B barks.

"What's up fellas?" I say stepping inside.

"Look who's back," Tone jokes from the dining table. Tone is cutting up a few ounces.

"Shiiit!" I respond shaking my head.

"Thanks for making that call for us to Christian," Tone announces.

"What call?" I ask.

"Christian. He about to get us what we need," Tone says.

"Treasure you know Reese?" B asks this beautiful caramel skinned girl. She is dressed like she works for Gucci.

"Yeah I remember Reese," Treasure says looking me over.

Treasure is Lamar's little sister. Well, I remember her when she was a kid but now she has filled out to be a beautiful grown woman. B told me that she's been in the game hustling with them since I've been out. I was surprised when I heard that but now I am actually seeing her at work. Treasure could be in any of these national recording artist videos or on someone's magazine cover, but she chose to be in the game instead. I give her a hug and proceed towards the fellas.

"So what are you doing in here?" B questions stuffing bags with money.

"I need to talk to you for a minute," I respond shaking their hands.

"Well hurry up. I have to go meet your brother to give him this money. That shit right there is all we have," B stresses, rapidly tossing bands of cash in the bags.

"That's a lot of dough," I say starring at the remaining stacks of money to go inside.

"This ain't shit for real. Heroin prices are dumb high now and it's hard to get some powder half of the time. Shit I wish I would have saved my money and gotten out of this shit like you did Reese." B replies zipping up the bags.

"Come on out here so we can talk," I express walking back towards the door.

"Okay."

B placed the bags in his trunk and tucked his pistol in his belt. I study his body language, and I am honestly feeling like I am looking at my past self in the mirror.

"Man, earlier I was with Christian and Keith, and Keith told me he found Simone," I whisper like people are trying to listen.

"Simone?" B questions.

"Simone man! Peaches! You know the bitch that shot me!" I shout.

"Wow! What you want to do?" B asks bracing himself against his car.

"I'm not going to do shit! Brah said he got it," I spat aggressively.

"Damn Christian has a lot of heart. He needs to be careful though. Those girls ain't out here playing."

"I know man. Please don't make me think about it. I told him to let it go but he wants them dead," I said formulating a response.

"He can't do it alone."

"I know. He's taking crazy ass Lamar with him down to Louisville."

"Louisville?" B questions.

"Yeah, that's where Keith's people found them. They said they were on their bullshit with them but they checked game before anything happened."

"Why didn't they kill them?" B questions again waiting for my response.

"Keith said they owed him a favor, so they saved them for me," I answer.

"Shit don't sound right to me. How about they are setting Christian up?" B says sounding concerned.

"Who Keith?"

"Man, I'm not saying that, but in this game, who can you trust? Who? The only muthafuckas I trust is right here!" B replies.

"I feel that, but Keith would never set us up. Not even my brother."

"I will talk to Christian maybe he will think twice about the shit, but if he don't, they need to hit those bitches right away. Don't give them time to think they're being set up."

"Yeah, talk to him man."

"I will see you tomorrow at The Roof Top."

"Yup. I'll see you there," I say walking down the sidewalk.

I drove off slowly in deep contemplation. I couldn't imagine the blood of my bother on my hands. I wouldn't know what I would do. Christian had his mind set on getting them back, and he is hard to persuade once he has been thinking about doing something. I could only pray for his safety and maybe have another chance at dinner to persuade him.

****

Early the next morning I am awaken by Diana's soft kisses across my chest. I look down, and she's sliding down my body in between my legs. Diana tugs on my boxers and pulls them off forcefully. Suddenly, I feel her tongue on the tip of my penis, and her soft lips hug me. I close my eyes combing my fingers through her hair. Diana takes her time to please me.

After I came, I didn't want her to feel left out so I swiftly flipped her over on her back and exchanged the favor. Diving down between her legs, I quickly take her legs and pen them back. All I see is a pretty shave pussy. I skillfully open her lips with my tongue tasting all of her juices. I tease her flicking my tongue over her clit knowing she's ready for me to handle my business. Suddenly, I feel her grab the back of my head signaling for me to stay on her spot. I scroll my tongue over her clit rapidly for a few minutes causing her thighs to shake like an earthquake. I feel her coming, but I continue to lick. She tenses up and screams. I take her hands away from me because she tries to push me away. Unable to keep her legs penned back, she moves her body out of my reach.

"Reese stop! I can't take any more!" Diana shouts in laughter.

"Damn, you are about to fall out of the bed," I laugh looking at her trying to get herself together.

"Come on. Let's get dressed," Diana says entering the bathroom.

****

Diana and I arrive at The Roof Top restaurant downtown. We are greeted by valet. Diana tips the young looking valet worker, and I take her by her hand into the building. I stare at her observing her beauty. So many years we have been together and here we are about to announce our wedding plans to our family and friends.

"What's wrong with you," she questions wondering why I am staring at her.

"Nothing. I am just thinking," I answer brushing her hair from her face.

"Turn to the side so I can see those sexy ass thighs," I say turning her.

"Boy, stop playing," Diana said.

"I just want to look at yourself before we go in here."

"Okay. I don't want you getting cold feet on me now," Diana giggles.

"Never. I want this more than anything in the world," I assure her walking out of the elevator.

On the way here, Diana and I wondered if everyone that we invited would come. I was more concerned to see if Christian would come because I wasn't so sure. When I spoke with him about tonight, he was so focused on Simone.

We walk around the corner from the elevators, and I notice a sign that has our names on it. Diana reserved a special section for our party. I heard the soft sounds of jazz music play becoming louder with each step. As we approached, I noticed familiar faces. Unbelievably, everyone we invited is here to celebrate with us.

Diana's father Mr. Gary approaches us with his arms wide open. He hugs her and tells her how beautiful she looks. After they speak, her mother hugs her and gives her kisses on the cheek. Moments like this I wish my mother was around.

Mr. Gary walks in front of me, "Thank you son for making my daughter happy. I really do appreciate all that you have done for her."

"Thank you sir," I respond.

"No honestly. I want you to know that you have my blessing, and I respect that you changed your life around for her and my grandson."

I never knew that Mr. Gary knew what I was doing in the streets. I tried to keep my affairs away from them so that they wouldn't trip on Diana for being with a dope boy.

"Thank you. I will do anything for them," I respond shaking his hand.

"I know that, and I love you as a son for that," he says looking me in the eye.

"Daddy what are you saying to my man?" Diana interjects.

"Just men talk."

"Gary come on babe," Mrs. Harris says pulling on her husband towards the rest of our guest.

We finally greet our guest including my boys and brother. I am surprised to see Christian and even dressed up like this was actually the wedding ceremony.

I hug my brother and friends. A team of waitresses come over with bottles of champagne and glasses. We all place our orders and share conversation.

Christian whispers in my ear that him and Lamar are going to Louisville right after dinner. I try to ask him not to go again but he is on it. I just ask him to be careful.

When our food arrives, Mr. Gary asks us all to join hands and pray. This was new for my boys and myself. We never prayed together or talked about religion much. We were always focused on our next dollar.

Before we dig in, I stand to my feet taking Diana's hand. Together we announce to everyone the reason for our gathering. Diana's mother and sister instantly start crying. I can't help but notice a weird look on Mr. Gary's face like he wants to say something.

Diana is suddenly interrupted when her dad stands to his feet and asks to speak.

"Baby, can I have the floor?" Mr. Gary asks.

"Sure daddy."

"First off, let me tell the both of you that I love you. I don't want y'all to worry about the wedding bill because I got it," Mr. Gary announces.

Everyone starts clapping but they don't take notice of the tears falling down his face. Diana tries to approach him but he stops her in her tracks.

"All I ever wanted was for my family to know God and to be happy. Reese, I know that you make my little girl happy and seeing her marry the man that makes her happy will mean so much to me."

"Aw, thank you daddy," Diana struggles from crying.

"Thank you sir," I say.

"I know that you both are not in a rush to get married, but I need you to think of a date within the next few months," Mr. Gary says taking his eyes off of us and onto his other daughter and wife.

"Why daddy? Is it the money? If you have a problem paying we will…" Diana questions with a concerned tone of voice.

I cut Diana off in mid-sentence, "Yeah Mr. Gary, I will take care of it."

"No, the money is not a problem!" Mr. Gary aggressively responds.

"Well what is it hun?" Mrs. Harris asks trying to read him.

"I went to the doctor last week for all of the migraines and blurred vision I was having. After some test, I was told that I have a tumor on my brain that they cannot touch," Mr. Gary cries.

"What!" Diana shouts.

"We will get another opinion," Mrs. Harris adds kissing her husband.

"That was my second opinion. That time I said that I was going to see my cousin in Cleveland and went to the Cleveland Clinic. I was told that I had three to four more months to live."

"No daddy!" Diana cries running to her father.

CHAPTER 3
CHRISTIAN

Lamar and I left from my brother's dinner and drove down to Louisville. We rented an Audi Q7 with Kentucky plates to fit in. My blood boiled through my veins, eager to get a taste of revenge. I had spoken with Keith before leaving to get his folks number so that I could get all of the information that I needed to find Simone and her friends. They gave me their phone numbers and the address to the place where they are staying. I gave Lamar all of the information and I watched how excited he had become. I know that when we catch them he was going to have fun.

Before we check into our hotel, we drive around downtown Louisville looking for someone that we can pay to check in for us. Not too long after riding up and down a few blocks we find someone willing to do it. The reason why I chose to pay someone because I didn't want anyone to know I was here, especially the police. I wasn't going to be a suspect in any case.

We enter our hotel room which is across the Ohio River in Indiana. The GPS says that I am thirteen minutes from the girl's location.

We quickly unpack and hide our show money. Time was of the essence. I don't want to risk the girls finding out about us or knowing that Keith's folks are on to them either.

I call Keith's people and find out the man's name is Kirk. I ask Kirk to tell the girls to link up with him so that we can stage a drug transaction. I want the girls to think we came down with a gang of money. He agrees to meet us at an abandoned apartment complex on the eastside.

Kirk calls me before we leave out of the hotel to tell me that he has it all set up. He said that the girls didn't hesitate to bite. He told them that he was meeting some guys from the Newburg part of the city to put on. Kirk stressed to the girls that we buy a lot of dope weekly and that caught the girl's ears.

Mar and I made a plan that he was going to meet with Kirk and his boys alone. I didn't want the girls to recognize me.

****

Kirk and Peaches road together in his European whip. He was followed by another car with two of his boys inside.

"I am glad that you decided to come with me to meet this guy. He be buying so much that I can't keep up. I will introduce you to him and maybe you can do business with him," Kirk discuss with peaches inside of the car.

"I really appreciate that. What do you need from us?" Peaches asks.

"All I want is for you to take a stack or two off each brick that I buy. He will buy eight to ten bricks every week or so. Sometimes we will link up in a couple of days."

"I believe that is fair especially if he is spending like you say," Peaches say staring out of the window.

"Yeah he asked how much I get them for from you, but I didn't give him an answer since we are just starting to do business together. I wanted for you to give him your own price. He has money to spend, and since my other connects don't have work like that, he can work directly with you.

"You think I can charge him thirty?"

"I don't know. He knows the game, so I don't think he will go for it but that's for y'all to discuss," Kirk says stepping out of the car followed by Peaches.

I keep my distance watching Mar meet up with Kirk, two of his boys, and Peaches. I wondered why her other friends didn't show. I figured they were out plotting on another lick.

Mar talked with Kirk briefly quickly making the transaction. Mar then steps towards Peaches after she calls him over. Peaches and Mar talk for a few minutes, and I notice him even flirting to make her believe he is fucked up over her and not focused on his money. Mar adds her phone number in his phone and climb into his ride driving away.

Everyone left the scene and Mar called me after he rode to the nearest gas station to tell me what was all discussed. Mar circled back and came to pick me up. Our plan was in motion.

Later in the afternoon, we meet up with Kirk at one of his spots to give him his dope back. We didn't sell any dope that wasn't from J. J continuing to keep that raw shit and my people loved it. We also toss Kirk twenty bands just for the look out, but he insists that we were doing him a favor and give us our money back. I respect him for that. Now I figured out how they are cool with Keith. Real muthafuckas fucked with one another. Shit after this I might truthfully help him out with my connect and get this money the long way.

Mar and I don't waste any time getting straight to our plan. In fact, while I talked to Kirk he was already on the phone acting like a straight lame. We wanted her and her friends to believe that he was a trick and a flashy type of guy. We wanted him to be an easy target for them.

Mar sets up a date at a restaurant downtown with Peaches. She gives him her address in which we already had and they made plans to meet. I honestly didn't think we would make contact with them so fast, but these girls were always looking for the next nigga to rob with their thirsty asses.

Before Mar went on his date, I remind this crazy ass fool not to kill her. He knows that Peaches was the one that killed White Boy and that was his boy. I had to remind him that he will get his chance once we get them all together then I will unleash the beast.

While Mar and Peaches went out on their date, I called a cab and had the cab driver drop me off in the girls' neighborhood. I wanted to watch their every move and study whose coming and going. My problem is that their house is in a nice neighborhood with a lot of elderly folks and families. Luckily, I was able to find a house that is up for sale, and I post up on the porch doing surveillance.

I wait for a few hours until I finally saw the bitch I came for; Simone.

Although I want them all to pay, I wanted to get her the most. I had taken turns with Diana at the hospital praying for my brother. Remembering my brother going through all of his pain trying to learn how to walk again was painful for me. I remember being at the hospital when Diana had Rico, and my brother couldn't even hold his new born son. I hated this bitch! She brought so much pain to my family that I wanted her dead more than I wanted my next breath.

Simone pulls into the driveway climbing out of a new Porsche Panamera. She pops open the trunk and takes out a gang of shopping bags. I'm just thinking that these girls are eating off of robbing dope boys. She don't have a care in the world, but little as she know, her days are numbered. I just need to get them all together somehow and I can put her behind me.

Cherish opens the door after Simone hits the alarm on her keychain. Simone closes the door. I continue to study the house for any additional movement, but the house remains still for another hour. Suddenly, my phone chimes, and I notice the caller is Mar.

"What's up family," I say into the phone.

"Yeah, the bitch believes I am out here showing out," Mar responds back laughing.

"Do she?" I laugh back.

"I told her that I will only be here for another day or two, and I wanted to get more weight before I rode out. She didn't hesitate to jump on it family," Mar said.

"Bet!" I say with excitement.

"Yeah, we are going to meet tomorrow night. I asked her to meet me at a business because I didn't really know her or her friends."

"You are on your toes boy!" I say eager to get their ass.

"Christian, I do this family. I'm going to have them meet me at the strip spot downtown. I don't know if you saw it when we were riding around," Mar speaks.

"Yeah, I think I know what you are talking about. Where is she now?" I ask wondering if she could possibly hear our conversation.

"She left about five minutes before I called you."

"Okay," I reply.

"You need me to pick you up? Mar asks.

"Yeah, pick me up on their street. I will be walking the opposite way of their spot."

"Cool," Mar says ending the call.

****

The next night Mar and I are in the hotel loading up our guns like we are getting ready for war. He tells me that he will meet the girls at the strip club and show them a good time. After that, we will catch them slipping and kill them. I wanted to get the girls outside of the city limits, but Mar suggested that we keep it near the city, so the killing would look gang related. He said that Louisville has a lot of "cold cases." I'd never killed anybody, so I take his expert advice.

Mar and I pull into the packed parking lot and find a dark spot to park. I sit in the car and allow him to go ahead of me. We want to make sure that the girls don't see me coming in.

Minutes later, Mar called me saying that it is cool to come in. I jump out of the car and flip my Ferragoma shades on. I have on a Cincinnati baseball hat to help disguise myself.

I enter the club, and I immediately see Lamar entertaining himself with the ladies. The ladies aren't acting scared to bounce their asses for them as he throws cash in the air.

I decide to sit at a table with a few beers and watch the scene. I don't know what to expect from these girls, but I know that they were just as a stone cold killer as much as Mar is.

Peaches and her friends walk in and take a seat almost directly across from me. I don't want to move, but I'm not sure if I sit too long Simone wouldn't recognize me.

Luckily, a dancer struts towards me, and I pull out a stack of cash getting her attention without saying a word. I ask her to give me a lap dance. She looks down at the money. Knowing I can't tease her with the money, I put two hundred dollar bills in her garter belt.

"Turn around for me," I ask for two reasons. I wanted her to block Simone's view, and I want to see her tattoos.

The stripper's tattoos are sexy as fuck. She has tattoos of lips over her ass and a long chain wrapped around her waist. She begins to slow wind on my dick then shift gears to bouncing on it. I am enjoying this lap dance especially when I get to watch her ass shake, but I have to keep my focus on Lamar and the girls. The stripper throws it harder when the DJ plays Young May Bishop's new single. May is a local rap artist in which the ladies as well as the gangstas loved.

I notice Peaches get up from her seat with her friends and take a seat with Lamar after he finally stops tipping the dancers on stage. After Lamar gives Peaches a quick hug, she takes a seat next to him. Peaches suddenly waves for her friends to join. Lamar asks for a waitress to bring them some bottles and the plan goes into motion.

I continue to watch Mar while I am getting the lap dance of my life. The dancer also brings her friend so that she can entertain me also. They are basically fucking each other right in front of me. I am enjoying the show, and they are enjoying the money storm. They allow me to touch them all over and even move their panties to the side so I can slide my fingers in. They ask me to meet them tonight for a real show, although I know that I was going to be busy, I took their number anyway. Mar suddenly get up and walks towards the restroom. I wait a moment, thank the ladies giving them another five hundred or so, and follow behind him.

Mar stands at the sink washing his hands, "Man, it's about to go down. They think I'm fucked up. They are on me like I am a king pin or something."

"So what's good? Do we continue with the plan?" I question waiting for his response.

"Yeah we continue with the plan, but we have just a slight change."

"What's that?" I question frowning up my face wondering what he has changed.

"I'm going to follow them to their spot and that's when you come in. I only need to get them all in one spot and that spot will be in the bedroom," Mar instructs.

"Mar, that is a little risky. We are taking too many chances to get caught or for something to go wrong. We should stick with the plan and do them now."

"Man, I know these bitches don't have you shook!" Mar aggressively replies.

"I ain't scared of shit man!" I shout but quickly get my composure when a man enters the restroom.

"I already told them I was coming, so if I change the plans, they will think something up," Mar says walking towards the door.

"Well, I am with it," I say walking out before him.

I take a seat at one of the bars near the exit and study the girls every move. Lamar was right. He has these girls taking body shots and playing with the dancers. They are ready or making him feel comfortable enough to get his ass like they got our people. I take this opportunity to go out to the car before he walks out with them.

Inside the car, I lay flat on the back seat out of sight. I can hear people talking around the car. I cock the hammer back ready to fire off on anyone. Suddenly, I hear Lamar standing next to the car and a woman's laughter. The passenger door opens and Peaches climbs in. She doesn't see me because I am now on the floor, but if she did, I would have blown her face off.

During the drive, Mar and her talk as if they have been knowing each other for years. There wasn't a pause in the whole conversation. I had to remain completely still because I didn't want to alarm her. Peaches tells him to pull into the driveway and that's when I knew it was show time.

I wait until they both get out of the car. I also wait to hear both car doors shut from Simone's car. Soon as I hear what I wanted, I sat up and got ready.

Mar shouts, "I have to lock my doors. I will be right in."

"Okay, hurry up. I have something for you," Peaches replies.

"Come on," Mar whispers opening my door.

"A'right. Here I come boy," I say struggling to get up because my leg has fallen asleep.

Mar walks to the back of the car and pops open the trunk. He takes out our tool needed for the job. We had planned on burying them after we filled their body with holes. The bag is filled with duct tape, rope, two assault rifles, and a shovel. I wonder why he is taking this in now, but I don't question him. The look in his eyes showed me that he is ready to kill somebody. I choose to keep my mouth closed and allow him to do what I brought him down here to do.

Mar walks towards the door like he means business. His walk reminds me of the business men walking Downtown Cincinnati going in and out of different buildings.

As we approach the door, he signals for me to stand on the other side of the door in the shadows. Unexpectedly, Peaches comes to the door swinging it wide open.

"You seriously carried all of that money with you?" Peaches giggles.

"Yeah! I wasn't going to leave it outside though. I can't take that kind of loss," Mar says sidestepping past her.

"You can put it over there in the living room," Peaches says turning and pointing in the opposite direction from me.

"Yeah, sit it over here," Cherish instructs patting the seat next to her on the couch.

I creep right in and grab her by the waist placing my gun forcefully against her temple.

"Can I join the party?" I ask provocatively.

"Oh shit!" Peaches screams being caught off guard. She drops her glass onto the floor causing it to burst.

Mar drops the bag and quickly pulls out an AK47 assault rifle.

"Bitch quit screaming! Y'all know what time it is!" Mar barks aggressively at

Peaches then storms off towards Simone and Cherish.

"What in the hell do you want?" Simone questions scared as fuck staring down the barrel of the rifle.

"You remember what you did in Dayton a few years ago?" Mar asks.

"Dayton? No. No. I never been to Dayton," Simone stutters. Tears rush down her face messing up her make-up.

"Bitch quit lying!" Mar shouts aiming on her chest.

"We never been to Dayton man. You must have us confused," Cherish finally speaks.

"Christian shut the fucking door! We are about to make a lot of noise in this muthafucka," Mar orders.

"Look, what do you want? We can get you whatever you need," Peaches interjects.

"Sit your ass down!" I say forcing Peaches down to the floor.

"Christian?" Simone cautiously tries to whisper to Cherish.

"Yeah, you remember now," Mar says nodding his head staring Simone down.

"No, I don't know him. I promise I don't."

"Now you don't know him. Maybe this name might ring a bell bitch," Mar playfully speaks.

"Who?" Simone cries.

"Reese."

"Shit that's what this is all about? I thought we killed him," Peaches asks.

Smack.

I hit Peaches dead in her mouth with the butt of the gun. Blood pours out of her mouth. She looks up at me like she wants to kill me.

Peaches spits out a mouth full of blood. Her teeth are covered with blood as she speaks. "Reese got what he deserved. They killed my friend and killed my man."

"That nigga is my brother, and he ain't dead! Reese didn't even kill either one of them!" I spat.

"Fuck all of that family!" Mar interjects.

"What is it y'all want?" Cherish asks.

"I am going to tell you what I want. First, I want to fuck the shit out of y'all then I want y'all to pay my friend back for his pain and suffering," Mar says pulling Simone's shirt with the barrel of his gun.

"What is that supposed to mean?" Cherish says looking at Mar concerned.

"Don't kill us please. I will pay y'all twice as much as he is paying," Simone pleads.

"Don't worry. You will pay what is due. Now get on your fucking knees!"

"What?"

"Both of y'all get on your fucking knees and suck my dick or the last thing y'all will see are these bullets flying into your body," Mar says sternly. He unzips his pants and throws the strap over his shoulder.

The girls crawl in front of Lamar and do what they were told. They both suck the hell out of his dick like their life depended on it. In fact, it did.

Peaches tries to offer her goodies, but I don't pay her any attention. I remain focused on the task at hand. All I want to do is kill these bitches and get back home to the money.

After a while, Mar orders for the women to get up and lead him to their stash. Simone takes us into her room. She flips over the mattress and behold stacks of cash. Mar forces all three of them to fill up shopping bags with the money.

Mar walks over to the mattress and throws it back down. He makes the girls take off all of their clothes and become completely naked. He slaps on a condom and chooses Peaches as his first victim.

Mar grabs Peaches by the hair and forces her to the edge of the bed. He wants her to suck his dick. Peaches tries to struggle away but her girls cry for her to calm the fuck down. Peaches reluctantly opens her mouth and Mar fucks her mouth as if it were some pussy.

Minutes after busting in her mouth, he punches her in her face knocking her on the floor.

"The next bitch that tries some funny shit, I will put a bullet in her ass! Do y'all understand?" Mar barks.

"Yes," Cherish and Simone says in unison.

Mar steps over Peaches' lifeless body and brutally rape the other girls. Mar punches them even when they are fucking him right. I believe he is getting off on this power trip.

When he finishes with the both of them, he walks towards the door as if the job was done. I have to snap him back into reality and remind him that our job is far from over.

Standing in the doorway of the bedroom, he looks over at the girls and blows them a kiss goodbye. He picks up his gun and shoots Peaches three times in the head without even blinking.

"No!" Cherish cries.

"Christian, please don't let him kill us. I have a little girl back home," Simone pleads pulling on my shirt.

"Get off of me," I say snatching away from her grasp.

"You should have thought about that before you got in the game," Mar says calmly before emptying the clip into both of them.

Mar shoots them point blank in the face making it hard for any coroner's office to identify them.

"Mar we were supposed to kill these bitches and get rid of the bodies. That was the fucking plan!" I shout knowing we had too much evidence lying around.

"Well, get rid of the bodies."

"You want me to drag out three dead bodies in the middle of the fucking night! Nigga you lost it!"

"I will be back," Mar replies.

"Where are you going?" I ask in a panic.

Mar ignores my question. He walks out of the front door, and I become nervous as hell. So many thoughts are running through my mind right now. I wonder if he was going to leave me here for the cops to arrest.

I rush into the bathroom and wash my face and arms rid of blood. I never seen anybody killed right in front of me. Frantically, I clean out the sink thinking I might leave a piece of DNA. While cleaning, I stop. I stare at myself and laugh.

Watching too many of those crime shows has me in here tripping.

Suddenly, I hear someone burst through the door. I peek my head out and see Mar standing in the living room. I hold firm onto my gun not knowing what he is up to. When I get to the living room, Mar has a gasoline container in his hand and a huge smile on his face.

"This is how we are going to get rid of the bodies," Mar smiles pouring the gasoline all over the living room.

"We're going to set the house on fire?" I question.

"You have a better idea?" He asks continuing to pour gas all over the house working his way to the bedroom.

"Hold up let me do something," I say stopping Lamar at the bedroom door.

I pull out my cell phone and take pictures of the girl's dead bodies. I immediately send the pics to Reese for proof that I handled these girls for him.

"What are you doing?" Mar asks frowning his face up at me like he became sick.

"Sending proof to my brother," I answer.

"And you say I lost it," Mar responds pouring gas on the girls.

Mar rips Cherish bloody shirt off and set it on fire. He tosses the shirt on their body and the room quickly catches fire. We rush towards the front door, but I notice the bag with our tools laying on the floor. The fire quickly reaches the hallway and the fire is racing towards us. I pick up the bag and rush out the door for the car.

Mar punches the gas and flies down the street like a street car racer. I turn around in my seat and watch the flames blow out of the windows.

Mar doesn't even look back once before we hit the interstate. He acts as if killing three women was all in a day's work. He gets on his phone and tells his sister to be ready to hit a lick of their own when he gets home.

This nigga is crazy, I say to myself.

CHAPTER 4

REESE

Bright and early the next morning, I am awakened by a strange noise. I roll over onto my side and reach out for Diana. All I find are cold sheets. Diana lets out a loud scream forcing me to sit up. The scream comes from the hallway. I climb out of bed and walk towards the sound.

"What's wrong? And why are you sitting in the middle of the hallway crying?" I ask trying to figure out the problem.

"Just leave me alone," Diana cries.

"Diana, tell me what's wrong with you?" I demand trying to pick her up from the ground. I look down and see the screen of her phone cracked. I know she ain't crying over a damn $800 phone.

"My mom just called me and told me that my father passed away this morning," Diana cries into my chest.

"Damn! He said that he had a few months," I say stroking her back.

"I know. Those damn doctors lied to him," she continues to cry.

"Diana maybe it was his time. God probably didn't want him to suffer. You always tell me to keep my faith in Him and you have to be strong and have faith," I say calmly.

"All he wanted to see before he died was us getting married. He told me last night that he was excited to walk me down the aisle."

"Babe, we are going to get married. I promise you that," I assure her starring her in her eyes.

"I know. I don't even want to have a huge wedding anymore. Just us and our family," Diana confesses in a low tone of voice.

"Baby, you are going to get everything you wanted. That's what your dad wanted so I will give it to you," I say sternly meaning every word.

"Reese, it's okay. Something small and inexpensive will be fine. I just want us to be married. That will make me happy and my father."

"That's my job baby," I say wiping her tears away.

Rico walks out of his room rubbing his eyes, "Mommy, why are you crying?"

"Mommy is okay baby. I am just sad right now," Diana says kneeling down to hug Rico.

"Why are you sad?" He asks looking her over.

"Mommy has to say good-bye to grandpa."

"Where is grandpa going mommy?"

"He went to Heaven. We will see him again."

"Then you shouldn't cry," Rico says walking away.

"You are absolutely right," Diana responds quietly.

Diana and I take Rico over to her sister's house before we head over to her mom's. Her mom is devastated and needs someone to talk to. Diana wants to be there for her mom and I understand that.

We pull up in front of her mom's house, and before I can put the car in park,

Diana jumps out. She rushes for the door. I put the car in park and then notice that my phone has been off since last night. Soon as I turn it on it began to chime. I check out my messages and see that Christian has sent me multiple picture messages. I open up his message and notice pictures popping up. I instantly feel sick to my stomach seeing pictures of three dead women. When I slide my finger to the final picture of Simone, I feel a sense of guilt. Although she squeezed the trigger on me, I didn't have it in me to do the same to her. I delete the pictures washing away my past. I stare at the phone and decide to send my brother back a message: *Man I am not thanking you for what you've done. In fact, I wish you wouldn't have done it. I wanted to put that all behind me and now I have to live with her blood on my hands. Christian I love you but I don't want nothing to do with this. Please don't have none of that shit come back on me. I have a family now, and I want to be here for them.*

Not knowing how Christian was going to take my long ass text, I just prayed that he understood where I was coming from.

I send another text but this time for Diana. I text her that I was going to make a run real quick, but I will be back in a few minutes.

Pulling up to the local corner store, I see a few fellas near the corner getting their money. I don't know them but they knew me. That feeling of importance feels good.

I step inside the store and shake hands with my home boys from Africa. They play with me all the time when I come in here thinking I am out here making plays again. I continue to advise them that I am now a business owner just like them. I walk to the back of the store grab me an orange soda pop and a bag of salt and vinegar chips.

Boom! Boom!

The sound of two gun shots ring outside of the store. I drop down to take cover along with the other customers. I quickly shake it off and stand to my feet. My ears weren't used to hearing gun shots anymore, and around here, it's an everyday thing. The last time I heard some shots was when Simone tried to kill me.

"Reese, are you okay?" The store owner asks holding his hand gun in his hand.

"Yeah, I'm good," I respond.

"Don't be scared," the owner jokes in his African accent.

"I won't be. This is still my city family. Ay, where are your cheap ass roses at?"

"Right over there. I hope you're not taking those home to our woman," the owner continues to joke.

"Don't make me shoot you with your own damn gun," I joke back.

"Soft ass."

"Man, give me my damn change. I will tell her you said, 'hi'," I say walking out of the door.

Walking up on the door of the Harris' home, I can hear cries. Today is a difficult time for the whole family but at least Rico really didn't understand. I wouldn't know how to handle it if my little man knew what was going on. I enter the house and follow the cries. The cries lead me to the sitting room and unexpectedly it's not her mother crying its Diana. Diana's mother is actually comforting her when I though that's what she came over here to do.

"Baby are you okay," I ask knowingly.

"No," Diana cries.

"Reese she will be alright. It's just tough right now for her," Mrs. Harris says rocking Diana like a baby.

"I understand. How are you?" I question wondering if she's hurting.

"I have to be strong. He is with the Father now so I will be fine," Mrs. Harris responds letting go of Diana.

"Okay," I say in a soft tone staring at Diana.

"What do you have there?" Mrs. Harris asks noticing the flowers.

"I had went to buy these for you," I answer.

"Well, let's get them in some water honey," Mrs. Harris says escorting me into the kitchen.

"These are very nice Reese," Mrs. Harris says putting the flowers into a vase.

"I am glad that you like them. It's just a small token. I am truly sorry for your loss, and I will do anything to help you in any way I can."

"That's great to hear that. I do want you to do something for me," Mrs. Harris adds before going back to the sitting room.

"What's that ma'am?"

"My husband was so happy to know that his oldest daughter was getting married. That was all he had talked about. I want y'all to fulfill that for each other and for him. I know that he will be smiling down from Heaven the day y'all jump the broom."

"We will get married. She deserves it. I love your daughter very much, so please don't worry I will make sure it will happen," I say hugging Mrs. Harris.

"I am happy to hear that. I have a number for the wedding planner right over here in my basket."

"Wedding planner?" I ask never hearing of such a thing. People who I knew got married in the church, in the hood or downtown, nothing too fancy or too expensive.

"Yes a wedding planner. My husband and I had a meeting over the phone, and she seems wonderful. She already has plans for the venue and everything. Just give her a call and go from there."

"Okay," I reply thinking of the money I am about to spend.

"Don't forget to call the woman. Remember this is for a lifetime. You can't put a price on love," Mrs. Harris says walking away.

****

Diana and I arrive home, and she continues to cry. Not even saying a word to me, she climbed out the car and rushed for the bed. I never seen her so devastated. Instantly, I remembered how I was when I lost my mother. That pain was immeasurable.

Sitting on the couch, I stare at the wedding planner's business card. I notice a web site on the bottom of the card. I pull out my phone and go to the site. After a few minutes of reading all of her services, I really knew that I was going to spend more money than I even had. I had to figure out how I am going to raise some money fast. All I have is the Laundromat and my house. Selling either one of those is out of the question.

The planner and I talk for over an hour. She told me all that was needed from me is a list of things Diana had to do like picking out her dress. The planner said sometimes it can take months for a dress to be shipped out from another country. I didn't know what the big fuss was about a dress she was only going to wear once, but I guess it is a big deal. We made plans to meet early next week. That was fine with me because I needed to make some money.

Noticing I was on the phone a while with the wedding planner, I decide to get up and check on Diana. I crack open the door, and she is knocked out. I assume that she cried herself to sleep. I feel so sorry for my baby.

Feeling my stomach ache from hunger, I decide to order Diana's favorite dish from her favorite Italian spot. I hope this may cheer her up just a little. I leave a note on the nightstand and ride out to the restaurant.

The host greets me with a smile and tells me that the owner would like to speak with me. The owner knows Diana and myself personally, and he tries to speak anytime we are here. We come to the restaurant at least once a week, and I always treated the staff well with a nice tip. The host escorts me to a nice table overlooking a fountain outside.

The owner approaches me with a bottle of red wine and two black boxes in which I assume is our food.

"Congrats Reese on the wedding. If you have not yet made plans on the catering services, I will be pleased to do your wedding for half price," the owner says.

"Thank you. No, I have not made a decision on that. In fact, I will let our wedding planner know, and we will definitely consider it."

"We can schedule a tasting," the owner offers.

"Diana will be so happy. You know that this is her favorite place to eat."

"Yeah, she tells me that all of the time. I remember her coming in here almost every day when she was pregnant," he laughs.

"Right. That girl couldn't get enough. Well, I have to go. Thanks again for the bottle of wine."

"No problem. I will talk to you soon," the owner says shaking my hand firmly.

Entering the house, Diana is sitting on the couch with a box of tissue and a half empty bottle of wine. Her right hand is full of tissues and left has a glass of wine. My baby has been home crying her eyes out. Diana's eyes are filled with tears and her nose is red from what I assume was over her blowing her nose so hard. I notice that she's on the phone so I don't interrupt.

Quietly, I walk over to the kitchen area and warm our food up in the microwave. Normally, I would have placed the food in the oven, but I am starving. I place our food on separate plates and pour myself a glass of wine. From the corner of my eye, I catch Diana signaling for me to bring the bottle over for her also.

I sit our plates down and begin to pour her glass. Just in the small amount of time I spent in the kitchen was enough time for her to kill her bottle of wine.

Diana kisses me and dives in. She continues to talk to her mother about the funeral arrangements. I overhear that her sister wasn't going to help them with anything and that really has Diana pissed.

Diana ends her call with her mother and shares everything that they had discussed. Her and her mother had to go by the funeral home and pick out the casket. Her father had a request to be buried with his favorite Ohio State football gear. He was a huge fan. We had that in common. Mrs. Harris had already decided on the suit he was going to wear. Mrs. Harris assigned Diana the job to get all of the family to come together for the after the funeral dinner. She loves to cook, but she will need help cooking for an expected large group of family and friends. From what Diana is telling me, the hardest part for her is to simply say goodbye.

I couldn't imagine taking on the responsibility of someone I loved funeral arrangements. When my mother died, I was in another world. I totally zoned out. Since Diana was the older child, she went ahead and took on the responsibility. I am proud of her.

As we talked, we finished off our plates and murdered the bottle of wine. Diana's tears of sadness transformed to laughter with a little help of good memories she shared with her father. I also shared some memories of him.

Diana and I change the topic of her father and started talking about the wedding. I asked her multiple questions on her vision of the wedding, so I can have an idea to tell the wedding planner. We are on the same page when it came to us agreeing on the venue, honeymoon, and food. We both agreed to have her favorite restaurant cater. We also wanted to have our wedding outdoors somewhere hopefully a roof top or a nice mansion. Diana wanted to go to Jamaica for our honeymoon, and I always dreamed of just leaving the states, so I agreed.

We both are feeling the effects of the wine. Diana gets a little horny when she drinks, but I don't wait for her to make the first move.

Diana lays back and closes her eyes. I position myself between her thighs. Slowly and gently I rub my hands over her thighs.

"Ooh that feels good," Diana says shifting her body just enough for me to get closer to her.

I continue to massage her thighs and feet. Diana goes crazy when I massage her feet. She is extremely ticklish. After a few minutes of a firm massage on her feet, she again relaxes.

Taking my attention away from her lower half, I direct my attention on her midsection. I look down at her fat pussy lips, and I decide to take it slow. I want to please her. Taking my eyes off of her pussy, I place them on her breasts. Her T-shirt is hanging off of her shoulder revealing that she is not wearing a bra. I lift her T-shirt up and caress her breasts gently. I simultaneously massage her breasts and kiss on her stomach.

"What are you doing?" Diana says in a low tone of voice loving my touch.

"Taking care of my woman," I reply continuing to work my way up her stomach.

I take her breasts and place them in my mouth. Swirling my tongue over her nipples, I feel her trying to resist, but I continue. I take my hand and rub my fingers over her clit and suddenly she lifts up.

"Reese stop! I can't do this right now!" Diana shouts looking at me like I did something wrong.

"Why not?" I ask.

"Not right now baby!" Diana cries.

"Baby, we are just getting started," I say reaching for her, but she jumps off of the couch knocking over the empty bottles.

"Reese, my father just passed away. Sex is the last thing on my mind!" Diana snaps with an attitude.

"Everything was perfect. Look at my man. He's ready. And you were getting ready yourself. I felt the pussy getting wet."

"Reese, you are a careless muthafucka! I don't want to have sex right now! I'm not thinking about any dick!"

"This shit is crazy!" I shout standing to my feet.

"Yes it is. You can't just be there for me while my family and I are grieving. That's fucked up."

"I am here for you!"

"No, you're not."

"I went out and got your favorite food to help get your mind off of everything."

"I don't care about any food! I want my man to support me and help me get through this," Diana cries picking up one of the bottles.

"I understand that but we still have to have sex."

"What! Are you listening to yourself? I can't believe that the man I want to marry is more concerned about getting his dick wet more than caring for his woman."

"It's not like that."

"You know what, since you want to bust a nut so bad, how about you and your hand get that shit together right here on the couch? I want you to think about the shit you said to me."

"You got me fucked up! I am not sleeping on the couch in my own house," I bark back.

"You won't be sleeping in my bed, and you want be getting any of this."

"Yeah, alright," I say picking up my car keys.

"Where are you going?" she questions walking towards me.

"If I can't sleep here, I will find somewhere else to sleep," I say slamming the door behind me.

"Don't come back either! You dirty muthafucka!" Diana shouts through the door.

Before I could open the car door, I hear her throw something at the door in which I assume was one of the wine bottles.

****

Opening the door to the Laundromat, I notice that there isn't anyone in sight but the manager. He is getting ready to leave for the night and close up.

"Hey, what are you doing here?" the manager asks.

"Got into with the wife," I say opening up the office door.

"I have been there before. Well, I am gone," he says walking out.

After the manager leaves, I flop down on the futon and try to chill. I turn on my favorite sports channel and relax. Suddenly, I hear the front door chime. I check to see who it is on the camera, but I can't make out a face. I did know that the customer was a woman. The previous owner had installed some high definition surveillance cameras.

Walking out of the office, I quickly notice the figure that was on my TV screen. Candace. I wonder why she came in tonight with only one load of clothes this late at night. Maybe she is a clean freak or maybe she wants to intentionally see me.

Again I study her amazing body and fantasize about fucking her. I don't cause her to notice me, and I allow her to wash her load of clothes. She doesn't notice I am here until she turns around.

"Oh! You scared me," she said shocked.

"I didn't mean to scare you baby," I say slick like a Chicago pimp.

"What are you doing here this late?" she asks walking up to me.

"I have to pay the bills. I decided to come in and get this money."

"You got some money," Candace says playfully.

"Why you think that?" I ask.

"You just look like a man that has money and using this as a front."

"Shit I wish," I respond.

"Are you here alone?" Candace asks almost whispering.

"Yeah," I answer.

"Why don't you turn off the lights," she says grabbing my dick.

"Alright, I will be right back," I say rushing off into the office to turn off the lights.

Before I leave out of the office, I notice that the cameras are recording. I watch Candace take off her tight jeans and throw them on a washing machine. I am shocked to see that she doesn't have any panties on.

As I approach, Candace takes her shirt over her head and turns around showing her petite breasts. She starts to take her bra off, and I step right behind her and assist. When I take off her bra, I am amazed how nice a small set of breasts look. I lick my lips staring at her erect chocolate nipples. Candace notices how I am staring at her and responds back with a smile. I can't resist myself any longer so I dive in to suck on them. I take each nipple in my mouth one at a time. While I am sucking on her breasts, she skillfully unbuckles my belt and tugs on my dick. It doesn't take long to harden fully. Within a heartbeat, she drops to her knees and sucks the hell out of my dick. She has me losing my balance from how good she is sucking. I brace myself against the folding table and relax. Candace takes my hand and places it on her head. I am caught off guard by this, but I don't take my hand away. Candace sucks on me until I release a shot of juice into her mouth.

Candace stands up and pulls me to her. She lifts up my shirt and place kisses on my tattoos. Like a seasoned freak, she jerks on my penis to keep it firm.

"Pick me up," Candace says looking over her shoulder.

I quickly pick her up and sit her down on the washing machine. I look down at her neatly shaved pussy delighted at the sight.

As I rub her thighs, she digs in her purse and takes out a condom then I knew it was on.

Again, she grabs hold onto my dick but this time a little more aggressively.

Skillfully, she rolls on the condom to the base of my penis then pull me in.

I enter her tight, wet pussy slowly with just the tip of my dick. Candace lets out a soft moan. Feeling her wetness, I inch in slowly feeling her lips open. Candace quickly grabs the back of my neck and positions herself for a deeper penetration. She wraps her coco legs around my waist. I slide in deeper and begin to thrust faster. Candace is taking the dick and riding it like a cow girl at a rodeo show. I pick her up off of the washing machine gripping her ass. Candace becomes more excited and works her ass in the same rhythm as I am. I take her ass and force it down on me and fuck her until she shakes uncontrollably.

Candace and I go at it for another hour or so before it was time for her to leave. When she left, I turned off the store lights and went back into the office after locking up.

When I sit down, I noticed that I left the cameras recording. I kick my feet up and watch the film like I was watching a porno. I have to say I did a damn good job.

CHAPTER 5

REESE

Three days has passed since Mr. Harris' funeral service. The funeral was beautiful. Diana and Mrs. Harris had him in a nice casket and the whole church was filled with flowers. Mr. Harris would have been proud of Diana and her mother.

Today is Rico's birthday, and although Diana is still hurt, she didn't want Rico to suffer not having a party. We discussed not having his party until later on in the month but Rico knew his birthday.

Diana and I called both of our family and friends to invite them for Rico's birthday party. Most of her friends had kids but none of my boys did. All of my boys treated Rico like their own son. They just knew he was going to be a hustler, but I wanted him to take another path - the same path that I had planned for Christian; school and maybe sports.

Diana and I rented out a hall to have the party. Rico is all into the animals and clowns so we decide to have this year's theme set up like a circus. We have animal trainers walking around with monkeys and snakes. The kids loved the monkeys. We had bought a popcorn machine with circus popcorn bags. We had another guy come in to make hot dogs at his stand. The theme is great. The party set me back four thousand, but the smile on my son's face made it all worth it.

B and Ashley arrived early at the party. Ashley helped Diana with a few of the decorations while B and I talked. I had to tell him about my night with Candace. B couldn't believe that I was back at my old ways and honestly telling him the story made me feel bad myself. I switched the topic quickly. I began asking him questions about the game and what's going on in the streets. B didn't seem comfortable talking to me about the life I left behind and I finally saw a gap in our friendship.

After an hour had passed, Christian and the rest of the crew fall through. These clowns get out of their cars with bags in each hand. Christian has bags and a bundle of assorted balloons.

We all enter the hall together, and before Christian could put his bags down, Rico is running to him with excitement. All of us laugh. Rico loves his uncle. Diana's single friend's eyes are glued on Christian.

Diana comes and greets the fellas and decides to announce that it is time to open the presents. Christian takes the microphone out of her hand and announces that he has a special gift outside.

Like a mob, we all go outside and a pickup truck pulls up with a trailer attached. The driver and a young boy climb out. They take off some straps that are holding down a box. The driver tells everyone to count to three. In unison, we all count, and they pull off the cover revealing a swing set. The older kids at the party start jumping up and down and shouting like they just hit the lotto.

"How will Rico play on that?" Diana asks giggling.

"I don't know, but it's his," Christian responds picking Rico up.

"Thanks Uncle Chris!" Rico cheers.

"I hope that you have someone to put it together, because I'm not braking any nails fooling around with it," Diana playfully jokes with Christian.

Diana makes Rico sit down and open his gifts. Ashley wants Rico to open the gift she bought for him first. Rico don't want to open the gift from Ashley because it is a small box. He probably figured the box was a baby toy. He reaches for a gift that Lamar had bought him. Rico rips it open so fast that I don't get a chance to see the gift wrapping. Rico's face lightens up when he see the gift. Standing in front of him, I am unable to see the gift. Rico turns the gift around for me to take a picture of him and I am surprise to see what he has in his hands.

Diana goes off, "No, you will not be playing with this! Mar are you crazy giving my son a gun for a gift?"

I look at Lamar wondering what in the hell was he thinking buying this for a baby. This fool thinks my son is going to grow up doing what we did or worse be like his crazy ass. He is nuts.

"What you don't like it?" Lamar laughs.

"I should punch you in the face boy," Diana says sternly.

"Rico, let daddy check you out," I say grabbing the toy gun.

Rico continues opening his gifts and Christian asks me to step away to talk. We go back out to the parking-lot. Christian asks me about one of Diana's friend's. I instantly become upset because I am missing my son's party for this bullshit.

The rest of the fellas walk out talking amongst themselves. B don't hesitate to pull out a blunt and spark it. Lamar and B begin to smoke. Tone comes over to where we are standing. Tone is looking at us with this goofy look.

"Christian, who was that little thick thang you had yesterday?" Tone questions smiling.

"Oh, that's my new chic," he answers brushing the question off.

"Man she was bad!" Lamar exclaims slapping hands with Christian.

"Fam, and her head game is unbelievable," Christian laughs.

"Who y'all talking about?" I ask wanting to get more details.

"Brah, this girl I met at the mall. She is cute, thick, can fuck, and the chic has her on money," Christian testifies.

"Damn!" I say amazed.

"Shit, soon as I leave here I am going to meet her. She knows some people that want to buy two bricks," Christian says taking out his car keys.

"Christian, you don't even know this girl like that to be making plays with her," I say aggressively staring him down.

"Man let me do me. I ain't stupid. I am riding with her just to go feel these niggas out. If they are legit, then I will be making some money."

"Respect the game brah," I add.

"I know the game. Shit, I am the game. I am in the game. Your ass is washed up!" Christian spat.

"Washed up. Oh yeah?"

"Yeah nigga!" Christian says getting in my face.

"Man, I should kick your ass!" I challenge balling up my fist.

"Man, y'all need to chill that tough shit out," Tone finally interjects coming between us.

Christian pulls his gun out from his belt and sit it on top of Diana's friend car.

"We can get it," Christian says pulling off his designer shirt.

"You need to chill the fuck out Christian before I take that opportunity and fuck you up! You are getting hot out here in these streets and that's when shit gets ugly," I bark.

"Now, you want to son me. I am out here every fucking day getting it. I got killas out here ready and a lawyer on deck. I know what the fuck I am doing out here in these streets!"

"Slow the fuck down G!" I say pointing my finger in his face.

"Slow down? I can't slow down cause the money keeps rolling," Christian says taking out a knot full of hundreds.

"What are y'all over here talking about?" B asks rushing the scene.

Lamar continues to smoke not a care in the world. He is just focused on rolling up the next blunt.

"It sounds like you are jealous big brah! Here take this! Maybe this will pay for the party. Shit, here take another band and make me the co-owner of that peace of shit Laundromat you have," Christian says throwing money in the air at me like I was on a stripper pole.

I try to walk away but his words dig so deep under my skin that I couldn't hold back my anger any longer. I ball my fist up and take a deep breath.

Swinging right pass B's head, I connect a solid punch to Christian's mouth. Blood squirts out instantly. He staggers back and then rushes me. We fall down on the ground, and he rapidly punches me in the ribs. I manage to get my hand on his neck, and I choke him. Christian sits up but continues with his punches. A hard jab hits me in the eye, and for a moment, I can't see shit. Quickly, I reach out for him, and with all of my might, I pick him up and slam him on the ground. Christian lets out a loud yell.

"Break them up Tone Diana is coming," B instructs Tone.

B helps me to my feet before Diana see's us fighting.

"What are y'all doing out here?" Diana questions.

"Here we come babe!" I shout.

"Hurry up. Your son is asking about you," Diana says walking back inside.

Everyone but Christian goes back inside. He hopped into his car and sped off.

We continued to have the party without Christian. Diana didn't voice her frustration with me, but I knew she noticed my eye red from Christian's punch.

Hours later, the party was over. Diana passed out big bags of candy and small toys to the kids as they left.

"Babe, I will meet you at the house later. Your mother asked me to take her home," I say kissing Diana good-bye.

"Oh, that's great baby. Kelly and I will finish cleaning up and then I will head home," Diana responds hugging her mother.

Mrs. Harris and I secretly drive off to meet with the wedding planner. The planner has three venues she wants to show us for the wedding and reception.

When I put the address in my GPS navigation, I notice that we have a minute of travel time. The travel wasn't a problem but thinking of a topic of conversation was. To my surprise, it wasn't a problem. Mrs. Harris and I talk about the party and how she sees Rico.

We arrive at a golf course near the air force base in Dayton. It's beautiful. The wedding planner walks out of the huge wooden doors to greet us. Her and Mrs. Harris share kisses on each other cheeks before hugging me.

We enter the club house, and I am amazed; the art work, the marble floors, the people, I never been around people like this or even stepped in a place like this.

"So, it's nice right?" the wedding planner asks noticing the amazement on my face.

"Yes dear, but we would like to see more," Mrs. Harris interjects.

After thirty minutes of walking throughout the club house and checking out the location, she thought it would be perfect for an outdoor wedding. I am amazed. I imagine Diana and I standing together sliding on each other rings.

"Reese, what do you think?" Mrs. Harris interrupts my fantasy.

"It's nice, but my main question is how much?" I answer.

"Reese," Mrs. Harris responds.

"What?"

"Well sir, this venue will cost us $9,000 for three hours," the wedding planner adds looking in her folder.

"Damn! I'm not trying to buy the place!" I reply irritated with the thought of how much I was going to spend.

"Mister I want to remind you that I was given a budget for $75,000. This venue goes up to $15,000, but I have a relationship with them so they will cut me a deal," the wedding planner says with concern in her voice.

"I need someone to cut me a deal. Who gave you that budget?" I ask knowingly looking at Mrs. Harris.

"If there's going to be a problem with the budget..." the wedding planner says but I cut her off.

"No there won't be any problem. We can continue," I add.

"That's my son!" Mrs. Harris says punching me in the arm.

We went along with the schedule. I followed the wedding planner to a venue Downtown Dayton that she had in mind to use for the reception. I have to admit that the place was nice. I can see all of our guests enjoying themselves there. The wedding planner said she had one more venue to show me for the actual wedding and when we pull up I am amazed.

We arrive at the art museum. The museum is set in the perfect location. It's not too far for our guests to travel, and the reception venue is only a 4 to 5 minute drive.

Walking inside, I am in awe with the artwork and dated pieces. The museum is very nice and spacious. As we walk around a ball room, the wedding planner discusses multiple decorative ideas and plans for the sitting areas.

I stand alone day dreaming the whole thing. As she spoke, images are popping up in my head. I can picture the whole wedding day including our wedding night.

Mrs. Harris and the wedding planner bring me back to reality when they mention how much all of their great ideas are going to cost me. The wedding planner asks me if I like the venues or if I wanted to see more in the Cincinnati area. I tell her that this location is fine. Mrs. Harris agrees. The wedding planner asks for me to give the museum a deposit of 5 thousand dollars to hold the date for us. I use my bank app on my phone and realize that I only have 34 thousand in the bank and that's only half of what I need for this wedding. I write the check and Mrs. Harris jumps up in joy.

I drop Mrs. Harris off at home and decide to make a detour to the bank before going home. Diana has called me several times wondering what I am doing but I lie. I tell her that I'm helping out at the Laundromat. She accepts my story and goes about her business.

At the bank, I ask to meet with the bank manager to get a loan. He sits down and run some numbers from his computer and tells me that I cannot get a loan because of my credit. I don't understand anything the man is saying. Credit? What is that? I know that I have 29 thousand in this bank, and I pay my taxes. I am trying to be the perfect citizen, but he is asking me for something I don't have.

Not able to get a loan from the bank, the only people I can turn to for this amount of money would be my boys. I call B and ask him to meet me at a chicken and fish spot on Hoover.

I wasn't waiting no more than ten minutes before B arrived. Climbing into his car, I don't hesitate to ask for a loan of 30 thousand. This dude bursts out laughing. He claims he doesn't have shit nor does the rest of the crew. He tells me that they have been spending more money than they can count which didn't make any sense to me. The whole purpose of selling dope was to stack up and get your life right. These fools are hustling backwards.

"Man you should ask your brother," B suggests.

"No! After what that boy said to me. I rather get back out here and get it myself before I ask him," I respond becoming frustrated.

"Maybe you should. The streets need you," B adds.

"Shiiit! I'm cool G."

"What do you need that much money for? Are you trying to buy another business?" B questions.

"No. I need the bread for this wedding," I answer.

"Damn! Thirty bands for a wedding!" B exclaims.

"No fam. I wish it was just thirty. Her mom wants me to spend seventy-five."

"Her ass would be putting in on it," B responds.

"Right."

"Well, what are you going to do? Are you going to cancel the wedding till you get your chips together?" B asks staring me up and down.

"Hell no! She's going to get this wedding. I promised her man," I say.

"Alright man. Do what you have to do," B says shaking my hand as I climb out of his car.

On my way home, Mrs. Harris calls me. She tells me that the wedding planner has booked them an appointment for Diana to try on wedding dresses. I try to sound excited but underneath I am pissed. I need to come up with some money fast.

I call B again and tell him that I made the decision to get back in the game. He is surprised to hear my decision. I ask him to make the call to J. He becomes silent for a moment and then tells me that J has went back home to his country. B says the only one with some weight out here is Christian, so I couldn't avoid him any longer if I want to get this money.

Christian doesn't answer his cell phone. Becoming furious, I speed towards the house without even checking my speedometer.

Suddenly, Christian decides to call when I am opening up my garage door. Diana looks out the door noticing I am pulling in. She waves and goes back in.

I tell Christian that I need his help with him throwing me two bricks that I could flip real quick for the wedding money. Not even arguing with my decision or bringing up the other day he tells me that he can get me together.

Christian asks, "How soon do you want these?"

"How soon can I get them off of your hands?" I counter.

"I can go get you what you need now," Christian says.

"Bet!" I say with excitement.

"Reese, I am about to pick up my girl that I was telling you about, but we can still meet."

"Where?"

"Let's meet at your spot," Christian suggests.

"Um, okay. I really don't want to be doing business around there."

"Man, it's the best place. I will be in the area and we can make it happen without any problems," Christian replies.

Closing the garage door back, "I am on my way. Give me like 15 minutes."

"That's perfect," Christian says ending the call.

I am inside of the Laundromat waiting for Christian for over an hour. I don't want to seem desperate but I am. I can't imagine letting Diana down.

Continuing to sit and wait, I become frustrated and even mad at myself for thinking about getting back in the game. Maybe something else will pop up with an opportunity to get this money, but I wasn't going to wait to find out.

I lock the door and get into my car. Soon as I start the car up, Christian pulls up. I signal for him to roll his window down.

"Man, I have been here waiting for a minute brah. You trying to play me like a sucka ass nigga!" I say angered.

Christian acts as if he is not even listening to me. He closes his eyes and cocks his head back as if he is high on something.

"Christian!" I shout.

"What?"

"Man, are you high?" I ask trying to study him.

"No, I am just busy. You should try to relax," Christian says with a smile on his face.

I sit up from my lean to stare him in the face and I see a fat ass poke up from the passenger seat. This boy is getting head while talking to me. I don't want to seem like a blocker, but I want to get this transaction on and over with before I changed my mine.

Soon as I slam my door shut and take one step towards Christian's car, the lady's head pop up. I lock eyes with Candace.

She looks up at me like a kid getting caught taking cookies out of the cookie jar. We don't speak to each other, and I continue to do what I came here for.

Christian closes his trunk giving me the sack with the four bricks inside, "Glad to see you back in the game."

"Nah brother. This is just for one flip only. I am done with the game family," I tell Christian trying to sound as serious as I could.

"The game ain't over," Christian says driving off with Candace.

His words stuck with me for a few minutes as I drove back home. The game has a way to get you when it wants you to play again.

Itching to look at the work, I decide to pull over at a fast food joint. I open the bag and that smell hits me again. My brother came through showing me love with four

and I didn't even ask for them. I smile
knowing it's time to go to work.

CHAPTER 6

CHRISTIAN

Last night was another wild night. After putting Reese on with a couple of bricks, Candace and I headed to her home. I was surprised to find out that she lived right around the corner from the Laundromat.

At first, Candace tried to keep me outside in the car, but she reluctantly welcomed me after I begged a few times. I wanted the opportunity to get in her crib and fuck the shit out of her.

We enter her two bedroom apartment, and I am stunned. She tried to tell me that her apartment wasn't ready for any guests in which I believed would be dirty. But to my surprise, her apartment look like it is staged for potential residents to view. I know that that furniture is new because when I set down a tag pocked me in the neck. This wasn't any cheap furniture either.

Candace rushed off into her room and came out with a large purse with her night clothes stuffed into it. I didn't know that she was wanting me to take her somewhere.

"Let's go get us a room," Candace announces walking towards the door.

"What's wrong with staying here?" I ask looking around the apartment.

Candace climbs on my lap, "I like having sex in strange places. Doing it here is boring. You like it when I bring out my freaky side don't you?"

"Yes I do," I answer.

"Well, let's get a room so I can show you more," Candace responds.

When we arrive in our hotel room, Candace gets a call from her people that want to buy five bricks from me. I met them earlier today, and they bought one brick from her. I didn't want to do the transaction with her people not knowing them, so I allowed her to sell it first. Now that I know that they are legit, I will do the next sell. I am eager to make a quick $100,000 and a $25,000 profit without making a sweat.

Soon after she spoke with them, she gave me the phone to finish off the conversation. I am trying to tell these guys where to meet, but I am trying to fight off

Candace from sucking my dick. Unable to fight her off while I am talking, she ends up winning the fight and take all of me in her mouth.

I couldn't take all of the sex Candace was willing to give. I mean she wanted to keep going soon after I busted a nut not giving me any time to get back right. I am happy to leave out of here headed to some money.

Candace and I ride to my stash spot in Springfield to get the dope for her people. She interrupts the music and asks about my brother. I know she was embarrassed getting caught sucking my dick in front of him. I told her that I was looking out for my brother and tried to play it off like he didn't see her doing her thing but she knew better.

Quickly changing topics, I ask her to give me her people number so that I can make sure that the deal is still on. She hesitated knowing I was trying to get myself off the subject at hand. Finally she makes the call and hands me over the phone. I take the phone and get right into business mode. I asked them to meet me at a grocery store parking lot near the hood. Since I was by myself, I wanted to meet them where I knew the area and familiar faces.

We wait in the rear of the parking lot which is perfect for me to see everything and everyone coming and going.

Candace looks shock when I pull out my pistol from under my seat. She doesn't say a word and begins to stare out of the window.

I take the five bricks out of a spare tire and throw them into a gym bag. Getting back in the car, I catch Candace talking to whom I assume are the people we are meeting. She ends her call telling them that we are waiting.

Soon after she put her phone into her purse, I notice a green truck pull up. It's the same truck that her people were in before so I knew it was them. They pull right alongside of my car. I keep the car running and climb out.

Opening the door, the driver shakes my hand and tells me to have a seat. He shows me the money, so I don't hesitate to climb in. I take a seat and crack open a brick so he can check it out.

"Do you want to taste it?" I ask holding the brick low out of anyone else sight.

"If it's the same dope I bought yesterday, then I want it," the man responds.

"Yeah, it's the same shit."

"Okay. Well here's the money. Can I hook up with you later this week?"

"Hell yeah! Just contact Candace and we will make it happen," I say exiting the truck.

Getting back inside the car, I am happy as fuck. I just made a bundle of money from a new customer without any issues.

"Let's go shopping," I say kissing Candace.

With my seatbelt locked, I put the car in drive, and before I can put my foot on the gas, police lights are coming from everywhere. Scared as hell, I punch the gas anyway. The tires scream causing smoke to fill the parking-lot. I swerve hard barely missing an undercover car. Several other unmarked cars race in my direction. Right before I exit the parking lot, I turn my head right and Candace has the barrel of a gun in my face.

"Pull the fuck over muthafucka!" Candace shouts from the top of her lungs.

"Bitch, what the hell are you doing? I don't have time to play with your ass! The police are right behind me!" I bark punching the steering-wheel.

"Bitch, I am the police," Candace snaps back showing me a DEA badge.

I take a long look at the badge, and with all of the strength in me, I quickly punch her in the face making her head bounce against the glass. Her gun drops in her lap. I take another look at her and then the badge realizing that I have been set up.

Behind her head, I see more lights. I speed off in the opposite direction of four police cruisers speeding in my direction. Candace body jerks from the power of the car causing her to fall against the dashboard.

Speeding through the city streets, all I see in every direction are police lights. I hit a corner hard speeding down a side street to get near my neighborhood. I know that if I make into my hood someone will protect me. I hope to make it to my Aunt's house, so that I could maybe hide out.

Finally reaching her block, I feel a sense of relief. Unable to see the bright red and blue lights in my rear-view mirror, I know that the police are close but not close enough. The sirens wailing, but I continue to speed. I glance over at Candace for a split second, and soon as I turn my head back around, I see a little boy around five or six run out into the street. I slam on my brakes and cut the wheel missing the kid, the car fish-tales; my rear end slaps the front of a parked car which causes my car to flip from the impact.

I don't know how many times we flipped but luckily we landed perfectly. The sirens are now loud as hell. I know the cops are close. I look over at Candace and she remains knocked out. Her face is now bloody from the crash. Almost the whole block must have heard the crash because everyone is out staring at me.

Feeling weak, I struggle to open the door. After three failed attempts to open the door, I get it to open on the forth. I fall on the ground knocking the door open. Looking up, I see my Aunt standing on her porch. I hear her yelling at me to get up, but I am so weak. I try to get to my feet, but I fall to my face.

"Put your hands up!" the man from the green truck shouts.

"I can't!" I aggressively shout back in pain.

"I am going to ask you again! Put your muthafucking hands up!" he shouts again.

On my knees, I struggle to stand, and when I try to obtain my balance, I feel some bullets hit me. The bullets force me to fall backwards against the car. My Aunt screams, and I see her running towards me. Her next door neighbor picks her up off of her feet carrying her away. The man from the green truck and other cops rush me with their guns drawn. I close my eyes and take a long deep breath.

CHAPTER 7

REESE

With Mrs. Harris watching Rico, Diana and I decide to step out. She just wants to step out and get a drink and listen to some music. I take her to a nice bar and grill on the north side of the city near the casino.

Diana confessed that she has been thinking to ask me to hold off on the wedding until we are cool financially. I try to assure that we will be fine, but she isn't taking the bait.

"How are we going to afford this wedding Reese?" Diana asks looking me up and down.

"I am going to take out a loan on the Laundromat," I respond back quickly.

She takes a sip of wine, "No Reese. We can just wait baby. I will start putting more money aside, and we can get married next year."

"Next year!" my voice grows louder.

"We just don't have the money babe. You know that I want to marry you more than anything, but I don't want us to be stressed over trying to make it the perfect wedding," Diana says taking my hand in hers.

"Listen. I got this. I don't want another day to pass without us being married for life," I say kissing her engagement ring.

"If you say you got it, then I believe you," Diana says tearing up.

Diana and I must have drunk enough to fill three or four wine glasses. She normally doesn't drink this much, so the alcohol has her busted.

We barely managed to get outside to the valet before she almost fell in front of everyone. I had the valet open her door to help her get inside.

By the time we arrive at home, she is knocked out. I park the car and carry her in. I carefully place her down on the bed and gently take off her clothes. As bad as I want to stir her juices up with my tongue, I decide against it and allow her to chill.

Diana won't be moving any time soon, so I take this opportunity to check out the two kilos of cocaine that I bought from Christian. It feels like it has been forever since I held a brick in my hands. I hold the bricks in my hands carefully like a newborn baby. I give both bricks a kiss before putting them back in a tool box that I hid in the garage. I knew Diana wouldn't dare check there for anything.

I climb in the bed and soon as my head hit the pillow I begin to think about my life. So many thoughts race through my brain. I remember when the crew and I first got in this shit. I think of the last conversation that I had with White Boy. I question myself is this all worth it. The dope game has only given me so much but has taken away so much more. Shit ain't the same.

Ring. Ring. My phone chimes interrupting. I check the screen and it's B.

"Hello," I say answering the phone.

"What's up? Can you get loose?" B asks.

I look over at Diana, "Yeah man."

"I have some money for you to make right now man. Meet me out front," B says ending the call.

B climbs in the car with me. We shake hands and drive off. I don't know where we are going, but I knew it pertained to selling these bricks that I have.

"Christian let me know that he got you together. I have a crew that need to get on. You can sell them the bricks for 25 a piece," B says.

"Damn!"

"I tried to tell you that it's bad out here family. Your brother has the game on lock. We are shipping shit all the way up to Cleveland and Indianapolis."

"Christian doing it like that?" I ask with excitement.

"I can't lie; he's doing it big. He has trap houses all over the state. With Lamar being his muscle, ain't nobody going to test him."

"I was wondering how he just threw me four bricks like it wasn't shit," I respond.

"Man, four bricks ain't shit to him. That man be getting a hundred bricks of white and fifty of brown every month. I guarantee."

B and I continue to talk about Christian until we pull up to a ran down high rise apartment building.

"We have to go in there?" I ask nervously.

"Yeah. It's on the 14th floor. Oh, you need a piece right?"

B pulls out a .38 pistol and hands it to me. Before climbing out, I check the scene. It's been so long that I still have jitters.

We enter the building passing by a crowd of dope fiends. I know that this spot is on fire, but I want to get this money by any means.

Stepping off the elevator, I smell strong odors of piss and mode. B acts as if he don't smell a thing. He bangs on the door and an old man answers. The old man opens the door for us and B walks in slapping folk's hands like he is a superstar.

B handles the whole transaction literally taking the bag of dope out of my hands. He only asks me for the ticket for the bricks. They don't argue and the old man gives me the money. I find a seat to count, but B insists that all of the money is accounted for.

We leave the building without any issues. I give B four thousand for the sell, and we pull off.

B asks me to take him to his spot off of Smithville. I agree just because I have a bag full of money, and I can pay for the whole wedding with just this one deal.

We pull in front of the spot and B jumps out. My phone begins to ring constantly, but I ignore the calls. Tone suddenly runs out of the spot heading towards us. Tone struggles to pull his T-shirt over his head while running. He has his pistol out and ready. I wonder what he is up to. B pulls out his pistol in broad daylight.

"What's up?" B asks.

Tone ignores his question and hops in the back seat.

"What's up man?" I ask.

"We have to get to the hospital!" Tone says patting my shoulder frantically.

"Why? What's wrong?" I question looking him in his eyes.

"Christian has been shot!" Tone shouts.

"What!" I shout putting the car in drive.

"By who?" B asks turning around in his seat.

"I don't know. I just got a call saying he is on the block laying in the street shot," Tone answers.

My phone blows up again. It's my aunt.

"Where are you?" she screams into the phone.

"I'm on my way."

"The ambulance has already taken him to the hospital," she cries.

"Who shot him?" I ask whipping corners.

"The fucking police!"

"What! Why?"

"I don't know they just gunned him down. I am on my way to the hospital now."

"I will be there in a minute," I say ending the call.

When we arrive at the hospital, all we can see are news vans and reporters along with the alphabet boys as far as the eye can see. I am wondering what did Christian get himself in to.

B leans back in his seat, "Reese I love your brother like we are family, but I'm not stepping in that bitch."

"I can't do it either bro," Tone interjects.

"So, y'all are going to wait out here?" I ask looking at both of them.

"No man. I am going to call Ashley and have her pick us up," B answers.

"Alright. I will see y'all later," I say running towards the hospital entrance.

Go to the emergency room and Christian is not listed. Frantically, I call my aunt, and she tells me that he is in there, but the hospital has him under a secret name to protect him. She gives me his name. I tell the desk nurse, and they allow me to go back to his room.

Walking towards his room, I see police scattered everywhere. A guard sits in front of my brother's room reading a newspaper. The guard asks for my driver license. I show him my identification, and I pass him by.

Entering the room, I can hear my aunt crying and the sounds of machines beeping. I am shocked to see my brother with tubes down his throat and a breathing mask.

My aunt rushes me, "Glad to see you boy. He has been sleep since I got here. They removed four bullets from his body, but I believe he will be fine."

"Yeah, he is a fighter," I say feeling myself about to cry.

Suddenly, a skinny Hispanic looking man enters. I know that he is not a doctor because he is wearing street clothes.

"Hi, I am agent Tony Rivera," he says flashing his badge trying to look tough.

"Agent?" I question screwing up my face in disgust.

"Reese, don't say anything to him!" My aunt says firmly coming between us.

He looks at me with this weird look that disturbs me. I try to stare him down, but my aunt is getting louder and louder talking shit to the man.

"Please calm down miss," the agent says calmly.

"If you want to talk to me or my brother, feel free to contact our lawyer," I interject giving the agent our lawyer's card as if it was mine.

The agent walks out the door, "I will talk to you really soon Reese."

"Shit no!" I bark.

As the agent is walking out, I am on the phone with the lawyer. Surprisingly, the lawyer is fully aware of the situation. He tells me to meet him at his office later and instructs me not to talk to anyone.

Before I leave, I give my aunt a kiss and tell Christian that I love him. I grab his hand tightly just to let him know that I am here. I open the room door and a news reporter rushes me. She tries to ask me questions but a city police officer stops her in her tracks.

Walking towards the exit, I see a nurse that I have known since high school. I run over to her and pull her to the side.

"Hi Reese. I am sorry to hear about your brother," she says sincerely.

"Thank you. I believe that he will be fine, but I need you to do a favor for me," I say putting my arm around her.

"Anything. Just tell me," she says looking at me up and down.

"I need you to keep an ear out for my brother."

"Reese, I don't work that floor."

"Shit!"

"I can have my friends keep an ear out for you."

"Bet!" I say with excitement.

"What do you want them to do?" She asks.

"I want them to tell me who's going in and out and most importantly be honest with me on the his status," I answer pulling out a knot of cash.

"They won't be a problem," she states taking five hundred dollars out of my hands.

I take off from the hospital heading to the lawyer's office. I don't know if it was blazing outside or if it is just me. Visions of my brother laying in that hospital bed, is driving me crazy. I have to find out why the police shot him.

Ring. Ring. My cell phone chimes.

Tone calls to tell me that the whole neighborhood saw what had happened to Christian. He said that Christian wrecked, and when he had gotten out of the car, the police shot him.

I ended the call and became even more furious. I wonder what could I do but going up against the police is out of the question. Maybe the lawyer has a plan to get these muthafuckas back.

At the lawyer's office, my phone constantly rings, but I ignore all calls because I want to understand what the lawyer has to say to me.

"Reese, have a seat," the lawyer says closing the door behind me.

"Thanks for allowing me to speak with you face to face sir," I say shaking his hand.

"How can I help you?" he asks taking a seat.

"I need some answers. People are saying that the police shot my brother."

"Your brother is in a lot of shit right now. Yes, the police did shoot him after they thought he was reaching for a weapon. Your brother took them on a high speed chase after selling some drugs to an undercover."

"Are you fucking serious man?!" I shout banging my fist on his wood table.

"Calm down!" The lawyer orders.

"We have witnesses that say they just shot when he tried to stand to his feet."

"Are these witnesses willing to take the stand against the police? I know how those residents act when it's time to testify."

"That's our neighborhood. We run those streets. I will definitely have someone tell you what they saw."

"The residents need to cooperate fully. They have to tell everything they saw from the beginning to the end. This won't be a speedy trial. This will take a lot of time."

"Man, my brother is the one in the hospital. He didn't deserve that. I don't know if he will make it."

"I also found out from my private investigator that a federal confidential informant told on your brother," the lawyer says taking his glasses away from his face.

"Who?"

"I will find out soon his name but be sure that he is well protected. In the meantime, don't do anything stupid and lay low," the lawyer orders.

"I don't even get down anymore, but I understand what you are saying."

"Reese, call me for anything," the lawyer says standing to his feet.

"Before I leave, can you push the issue for the police not question him or anyone in my family?"

"I sure will. I will have them release the evidence they have against him, preferably the tape of the shooting if possible."

"Thank you sir," I say leaving the lawyer's office.

After leaving from the lawyer's office, I am so paranoid that I refuse to talk to B over the phone and decide to meet him at their spot.

B, Lamar, and Tone meet me at the spot. I tell them exactly what the lawyer just told me minutes earlier. Everyone is nervous but Lamar. I don't understand why but that fool is nuts anyhow.

I tell them to leave the game alone just until Christian beats this case in court but all of them begin to mumble and groan. I don't understand how hard it is to stop just until the feds figure out that they don't have anything on us.

I know that I wasn't going to touch another gram of dope for any reason. They have a choice to make. I made mine.

CHAPTER 8

REESE

With everything going on, I decide today to spend some family time with Diana and Rico. We want to have a nice day together riding around and enjoying the spring weather.

Without a set location to go, Diana asks to go to the mall and get Rico a few things. A few things always meant a whole day of shopping but it was cool. Diana and I love shopping together unlike most couples. We have similar tastes in clothing, and I sometimes add my input when she purchases heels. We both share the taste for expensive designer clothes, so we make sure Rico has the same.

We have been in the mall shopping for almost three hours. We order some Mexican food and have a seat to eat. While we are sharing conversation, my phone goes off. I ignore the call but that does not stop Diana from smacking her lips and eye balling me.

Not waiting to hear her mouth, I pull out my cell phone and check to see who has been blowing me up. I have missed calls from B and my aunt.

Believing that B doesn't want anything, I call my aunt because I know that she has been spending time out there with my brother.

She answers on the first ring, "Hey. I wasn't bothering you, now was I?"

"I am out with Diana and Rico at the mall. What's up?"

"I was just sitting here wondering did you ever get in contact with the girl that was in the car with Christian? I think they took her to jail because the police put her in back of a police car."

"Christian was riding with somebody when he wrecked?" I question walking away from Diana and Rico.

"Yes! She was in the car. The paramedics checked her out for a second then the police took her away."

"Damn! I don't know who that could be. You know that boy keeps a girl with him."

"Not when he is working," my aunt snaps back with an attitude.

"Are you sure it wasn't Mar's little sister Treasure?" I ask believing it could have been her.

"No! I know who Treasure is Reese," she says sarcastically.

"A girl? If it wasn't Treasure, then I don't know."

"Reese you need to find out. Whoever she is she can be singing like a bird right now telling everything she knows."

"I am on it auntie."

"Reese, try to come down here and see Christian today. They say people can still hear you when they are out."

"I will come through later. I have to make a run to the Laundromat. Shit! Fuck!"

"What!" My aunt shouts into the phone.

"Reese, are you okay?" Diana asks walking towards me.

"I know who the girl is!" I shout figuring who she is. I run over to the table to pick Rico up.

"What girl?" Diana asks staring me down.

I hold up a single finger telling her to wait one minute.

"Who is she?" My aunt asks frantically.

"Her name is Candace. I think I know where to find her. I will be there later. I have to go."

I end the call with my aunt and explain everything to Diana as best as I could during our drive. Diana insists on riding with me but I disagree.

Leaving the house, I fly to the county jail downtown. I ask the clerk about Candace and the clerk cannot find a record of her. I am so confused.

Suddenly, I think about the last time I seen Christian before the wreck, and she was with him. Her face smashed down in his lap. I ask myself, *was she getting close to me so that she could get into my brothers pockets*? Shit, maybe even a worse scenario, maybe she is one of Simone's friends looking for her taste of revenge. All I know for sure was that she wasn't any good for anyone of us, and she has to be dealt with.

After leaving the jail, I rush off to the Laundromat. Dennis is sitting on one of the benches watching television. I pull on his arm getting him away from the customers. I don't want them to hear our conversation.

"Dennis. A man, you remember that girl that comes in here like every Sunday? I ask panicking.

"Yeah, Candace."

"You said you know where she lives right?"

"I think she stays at those apartments around the corner. She drives a new Charger. I believe it's either blue or black."

"Yeah, it's black."

"Okay."

"The apartments right up the street? Okay that's all I need."

Running out of the Laundromat, I rush to get into my car. I speed off up the street and find the apartments in which

Dennis mentioned to me. The apartment complex is large, but I found her car without any difficulty.

Parked behind her car, I sit and wait for her to come out. I am hoping to catch her slipping so that I can ask her a few questions myself.

I eat a whole bag of sunflower seeds finally noticing that I have been waiting for her to come out for over an hour. Not knowing which apartment she stays in, I studied all four of them like a private investigator then I thought I should call the lawyer and ask him for the private investigator's phone number. I am willing to pay almost any price for his services. Candace can't just disappear, and if she did, I am going to find out where.

Without any hesitation, I call my lawyer, and not discussing why I need the private investigator's number, he gives it to me. I was surprised that the lawyer came through on his word.

The investigator tells me that he works for my lawyer so his fee is already paid. I am delighted. The investigator is an ex-cop, so he still has ties with a lot of cops on the force and federal agents. He said he will have some information for me in a day or two before we ended our call.

Continuing to sit in front of her apartment, I become restless. I decide to get out of my car. I slowly walk past her apartment trying to look in her windows. I am unable to see anything, but I do hear a television coming from her front door. I walk around back of the building and a motion light pops on. I hide in the shadows and make my way back around front. I sit back inside of my car and wait again.

Suddenly, red and blue lights circle throughout my car. I carefully reach for my wallet because I know the police are on one.

The cop walks up on my car and gives me the normal run down. He asks for my license and insurance. I hand him both items without looking his way.

The cop must have ran my information and saw the previous trafficking cases I had a few years ago. He approaches the car this time with his gun drawn. He orders for me to get out of the car. I wonder why he is being so aggressive forcing me onto the hood of his car to pat me down. Not finding anything on me, he puts me in the back seat. I notice my information on the computer screen as he drives off.

I repeatedly ask the officer why he arrested me but he doesn't answer until we are pulling into the garage. He tells me that I am arrested for trespassing. *Bogus*, I thought. The garage door closes, and he climbs out to get me. I notice a county transportation van loading a chain of inmates onto the van. I shake my head of the idea that I will be one of them again. I am not going back!

I am booked in and the deputies place me in a holding cell. I have to step over an old man sleeping on the floor using toilet paper for his pillow. Everyone in here I damn near know. They all are asking me how much they catch me with and who else did the police bag. They are surprised to find out that I am in here on some bullshit. People always assume the worst.

After eating an old ass apple and a cheese sandwich, two deputies come and escort me to an interrogation room. I repeatedly ask to call my lawyer but they ignore my request slamming the door behind me. I am pissed because I know I have the right to a lawyer.

Thoughts of why I am in here race through my mind. I am being held on a petty ass charge, so I don't understand why I am in an interrogation room.

Suddenly the door slowly opens, and I see a hand on the door knob. Whoever it is, is talking to another cop in the hallway about going out to a bar after work. The man's voice is very familiar. I can't put his voice to a face. I patiently wait to see his face.

The door finally opens and Agent Rivera enters. He gives me a stern look and throws down a folder on the table.

"I told you that we will be seeing each other soon. There isn't anyone to save your ass now boss man," he states pushing a chair violently.

"Is that supposed to scare me?" I joke.

"Tough guy, huh?"

"Man, get the fuck out of here and get me my attorney. I told your bitch ass that I wasn't talking to you before."

"You will talk either now or later!"

"Nah, I don't even speak your language," I say turning my head looking at the two way mirror.

Agent Rivera opens up the folder and passes over pictures of Christian.

"Yeah, we got his ass and your next. Your brother is looking at 20 years, and from what I am told, he is the underboss. You are my big fish to catch."

"Man, get the fuck out of my face with that bullshit!"

"You're next muthafucka," Agent Rivera says smoothly.

"Oh yeah? Y'all don't have anything on me. I haven't been in the game for years. Get the fuck out of here."

My attorney burst into the room interrupting our conversation. Agent Rivera is caught off guard. He pulls me up from the arm and orders a deputy to release me. The deputy looks at the agent but proceeds to uncuff me. I smile at the agent knowing he is pissed off.

"I won't be able to help you later," The agent says remaining to stay in the interrogation room.

My lawyer and I ride around the corner to a bar and grille to discuss everything that is going on. We take a seat at the bar and order a few drinks. He digs inside of his briefcase and pulls out what they have on Christian. While I am reading Christian's indictments, a fat dark skinned man takes a seat with us. He introduces himself as the private investigator. I shake his hand firmly. He pulls out a picture of Candace coming out of her apartment.

He asks, "Is this who you're looking for?"

"Yes that's her!" I say eager to know where she is.

"Well my man, I hate to tell you that she is an undercover DEA agent," he says pulling out more pictures.

The both of them are talking, but I am zoned out looking at multiple pictures of her wearing police uniforms and fits. He has a picture of her behind a table full of drugs showing her first multi-million dollar drug bust. I feel so stupid.

"Far as I know they don't have anything on you. They have been watching your Laundromat. They believe that you are using that business as a cover up." The investigator says breaking my thoughts.

"What? I don't do anything there or near there. Shit, I haven't fucked with any dope since I was shot."

Just then I think about what my manager Dennis said about Candace taking pictures in the Laundromat. That bitch wasn't taking selfies! She was doing surveillance on me. Slick bitch.

"Reese, I want you to lay low. Take your family on a vacation or something," my lawyer interjects closing his briefcase.

"I can't do that. Actually, my lady and I are going to get married in a month."

"Congrats," the lawyer says shaking my hand.

"I know that it's going to be hard but try to stay out of the hospital for a few days. You don't want to run in with the police again accidently. They will be watching your every move from now on, so if you're not done dealing now, should be your get out of jail free card," The investigator speaks.

"Man on my momma, I am finished."

"Reese, I will do my part and making sure no charges are filled on you for the trespassing. Please don't affiliate with anybody that continues to deal or talk on your phone about the whole situation. Any evidence can hurt your brother's case or build one against you," The lawyer instructs firmly.

"I believe that Agent Candace Jackson took the case because of the informant but was using you to get to your brother," the investigator adds.

"Informant?"

"Yes, they have a federal informant working against you guys. I will find out who it is shortly. They try to keep their name on the hush until we go to court. You know to protect them," The investigator states.

"Protect a snitch!" I bark aggressively.

"That's how it works. They bust a dealer to use them to set you up," the investigator says downing his bottle of beer.

"Sir, the agent said that he was going to give my brother at least 20 years, is that true?" I ask desperate to know.

"The charges he is facing add up to a max of 20 years, but I can probably get those charges shortened to a minimum sentence if he pleads guilty."

"So he will have to do some time?"

"Yes, but allow me to work on it."

"Man, my brother can't go to the feds."

"I will work on it. In the meantime, focus on your family and your business."

"You know what? I have something that can help Christian out!" I shout causing some customers to look in our direction.

"What's that?" The lawyer asks.

"You won't believe it but I have a video tape of us having sex in the Laundromat," I whisper.

"Damn boy, you're good!" The investigator says hitting me in the arm.

"Will that help?"

The investigator continues to laugh.

"It will help, but it will also put you in it," the lawyer responds.

"Anything for my brother man," I say standing to my feet shaking the men hands goodbye.

CHAPTER 9
REESE

Today Diana and I meet with the restaurant owner to decide which foods were going to be served at the wedding reception. I am in another world. I have not been up to the hospital to see Christian in a week. I was tired of seeing my brother struggle just to live. It truly hurts watching him struggle with every breath, but he continues to fight.

"Reese, are you coming in?" Diana asks already standing outside of her door.

"Yeah babe, I am right behind you," I reply climbing out the car.

Diana tries all of the food she knows she likes but wants to eat it all anyway. I am not truly focused on this tasting because my mind is elsewhere.

Last night B and Tone called me saying that their spot got raided. They were even more mad about other spots that they were having others hold down for them being hit. They said that they had taken a loss on at least a half million dollars in product and cash. Now with the news broadcasting each bust, it's putting more pressure on the police to capture everyone that is in the city dealing.

I didn't know what to tell them about their unfortunate loss but that is the game we play. Tone didn't like the gut hard truth, so he hit me back accusing my brother of snitching. I almost went through the phone on him. I wanted to punch him dead in his mouth.

Those words in the street are deep. If anyone is accused of snitching, it stays with them for life. I remind Tone that Christian is in the hospital all fucked up and hasn't said a word to anybody. Shit, how can he with tubes running down his throat? He has been out like a light. I wasn't going to have my brother's name in the mud but that's easier said than done. I finished off the conversation by hanging up on him.

Diana feeds me shrimp and steak to pick from. I choose the steak, but as soon as I did, the look in her eyes told me that she wanted me to pick shrimp. I try to change my answer with the chef and wedding planner but Diana interrupts. She tells everyone that we want both. I put on a fake smile because I knew that this was just the beginning of the marriage in which I was going to have for life.

The wedding planner reminds Diana that she has an appointment with the wedding shop. I also have to meet with B at the tuxedo shop. I give her a kiss and I leave out.

****

B, and Tone meets me at the men's clothing store, but I am confused as to why Lamar is not here. He knows that he is a part of the wedding party.

"Where is Lamar?" I ask stepping near the store entrance.

"We haven't heard from him," B answers.

"He might be in Columbus making some money," Tone finally speaks looking away from me.

"Probably."

"Yeah, he is making money off of Treasure's dude," B says nodding his head in agreement.

"We good Tone?" I ask not knowing if it was about to go down right here.

See, sometimes it's the ones you call family that will close your casket. Nobody can be trusted in the game.

"Yeah, we cool homie. We made it from the mud family," Tone says hugging me smiling from ear to ear.

"Bet!"

"Cut that soft shit out niggas. Let's go in here and get this fool his tuxedo," B interjects walking inside.

We are being tailored for our tuxedos and they continue to talk business around the tailors. I try to change the topic many times, but these guys are only focused on business. Suddenly, my phone rings, but I don't recognize the number. I think that it's the feds with this strange number, but I answer anyway.

"Reese, they need you down here at the hospital," my aunt says.

"Who?"

"The doctors. They are ready to pull the plug on him," my aunt cries.

I knock the tailor's hands away from my waist. B must have heard the fear in my voice because he stands right next to me.

"They can't do that!" I shout having my eyes tear up.

"They said that there isn't anything left for them to do. They said he's not getting any better, and he is suffering."

"I am on my way! Tell those muthafuckas to fucking wait!" I bark running out the store in my boxers and a suit jacket.

****

While driving towards the hospital, the nurse that I gave my number to calls me. She confirms what my aunt previously said.

I don't know how I made it at the hospital driving the way I did but I did. I park directly in front of the emergency room door and dart out.

I run through the sliding emergency room doors and head for the elevators that would take me to the ICU floor. I am jumping up and down like I am on fire waiting for this damn elevator. While having my nervous breakdown, I feel a sense of relief when my eyes meet the stairs sign.

I am jumping two steps at a time all of the way to the seventh floor. Tired as fuck, I still manage to have the energy to push the door open with force.

Only a few feet away, I see my aunt run out of the room crying. I start to run for her yelling her name, and security blocks me from the door. I push one security guard hard in the chest and manage to slip out of the others grasp. I open the door, and the doctor is walking towards me.

"Sorry. He's gone," the doctor says trying to step around me.

"What you mean he's gone? He's right there!" I say crying furiously.

Security finally makes their way inside and ask me to leave. I refuse. I want to talk to him one last time.

"Can I just see my brother man?" I ask.

"Get your hands off of him before we break them off!" B orders walking behind the security.

The security let go. I rush in moving the curtain away. Taking giant steps I leap towards Christian. Almost like slow motion, I fall to my knees seeing him resting. His eyes are closed, and I know he's not breathing anymore. The sounds from the machines are now silent. My heart is heavy.

I grab his hand and hold it tight hoping to feel him shake my hand one last time. Tears rush down my face like the Colorado River.

"Come on bro," Tone says picking me up.

I push Tone away aggressively not wanting to let go of his hands.

"Reese, he's gone family," B says calmly.

They take me out of the room. As they pull me out of the room, people are going in to take Christian out also. I cry like a baby knowing that my little brother is not here with me anymore.

CHAPTER 10

RESSE

Leaving the funeral parlor, I sick to my stomach knowing that I am making plans to burry my brother. I am more sane now then I was with my mother. I believe I am handling his death well because I have Diana's help.

Diana has been helping with calling distant family members in Texas, New York, and Virginia. Most of them knew because my aunt has been on the horn. It's just wonderful to have her handling things for me in my time of need. Diana also has been helping out with the Laundromat and making sure that I am not stressing over anything, but I am.

With Christian's funeral expenses and the wedding, bills are adding up real fast. I don't want to alarm Diana about these bills, so I give B the rest of Christian's dope that he had stashed to make some money. I could have made the deals myself, but I knew the people were watching.

After meeting up with B, I go home. Today was long and tiring. Picking out burial plots, caskets, and his last outfit weighed too much on my mind.

Laying in my bed, images of my brother and all of the pictures that had been put in my face appear. In my sleep, I can feel myself tossing and turning. I quickly sit up in the bed scared. I saw myself in my brother's casket. My heart is beating rapidly, and it's hard for me to catch my breath. I take five deep breaths to make myself calm down. *Why am I bugging out?* I ask myself.

I walk to the kitchen and pour myself a glass of water. I take a few sips, and suddenly, I hear a car door slam in front of my house. I creep in the living room and peep out of the curtains, but I am unable to see anything.

"Reese, are you okay?" Diana asks walking into the room.

"Yeah babe, I just thought that I heard something," I answer.

"I didn't hear anything. Come on to bed," she pleads.

****

Diana, Rico, and my aunt ride in the funeral home limousine on our way to the grave site. B and the other fellas chose not to attend the funeral because they all found a way to see him before the wake. Everyone has their way of grieving.

We park at the cemetery, and we exit the limo. The smell of freshly cut grass fills the air. I slowly step out feeling like I have ankle weights on. Rain drops pounce on my shoulders. I notice the men carrying my brother to his final resting place in a hurry trying to get out of the rain and under the green tent. I take a moment to get myself together and then begin to walk towards the casket.

Rico takes my hand, "You okay daddy?"

"Yes son. I am cool," I answer rubbing my eyes.

The family and friends gather around and listen to the pastor preach. He reminds me that this life is not our final resting place. I have to get my life on track. After that dream last night, I know that I want to be here with my family longer.

They began to slowly drop my brother down into the dirt and our family

145

and friends start to leave for their vehicles. I look behind me and notice faces that I have never seen before. I pretty much know all of his friends. These faces don't look friendly anyway. They look like cops. I know that they are cops. Why are the cops here?

After the funeral, we had a dinner over at a party room near our neighborhood where we grew up at. The party room is thicker than I had expected. I mean as far as the eye can see I see hustlers from back in the day to the ones that are getting money now. Mostly everyone has a shirt with Christian's face on it. Cars are lined out in front of the party room like a national car show. I am not surprised for the amount of love my brother has. He showed love to a lot of people even when he wasn't out here hustling.

Again throughout the crowd I see the unfamiliar faces; the police. They stand from a distance watching my every move.

We leave after several hours of celebrating Christian's life. My aunt put a ton of leftover food in my car from the party. I decide to take the food down to the men's homeless shelter.

Entering the shelter I recognize an old friend of mine. He used to get money with us back in the day. His name is David. David is a big dude. Looks like a starting pro football player. David used to rob other dealers from surrounding cities and neighborhoods for anything he could get his hands on. He was shot on a deal gone wrong and was busted with dope on him. He had to do twelve years in federal prison. Federal prison made him even more of an animal now than ever before. He just came home about a week ago and don't have a place to stay. I give him two hundred dollars and my phone number. I thought that I could give him a job working at the Laundromat fixing the machines and save me a buck. Besides, I wasn't using the office anymore to sleep away from home.

Before I leave, he thanks me for the job and place to live but offers me some jail house talk. He tells me that he heard from one of his cell mates that Christian was set up by a jail house rat. I knew that but what catches my ear is that the rat didn't just have information on Christian but my whole team including Keith.

Immediately after leaving the shelter, I call the private investigator to ask if any new evidence came up on me. He said no but the case is still open. He said that he will have the informant's name by tomorrow. I was so happy to hear that. I was going to make sure that whoever this informant is wasn't going to talk either voluntarily or by force. I was going to put Lamar on that job.

CHAPTER 11

REESE

The night before the wedding has arrived. Diana and her friends are at the hotel getting their hair prepped for the wedding. Diana and I agreed on not having any parties but B had other plans.

He booked a night at Keith's strip club only for us and our friends. When he told me, I wasn't surprised. I just didn't want the word to get back to Diana about us partying with some girls.

Diana has been playfully asking me if I am going to stick to our agreement, and I have answered yes without a smile on my face. Diana doesn't believe a word coming out of my mouth. She puts her ass against me and pretends to be a stripper dancing on me. It's funny how she thinks she knows my boys and I so well.

B knocks on my hotel room door. I look out of the peep hole, and he is ready with a bottle of Patron. Opening the door, he rushes in and attacks me.

"It's time to see some titties!" B says dancing with the Patron bottle.

"Man, what did you tell Ashley?" I ask.

"What do you mean, what did I tell Ashley? Shit, I run my house."

I take the bottle from his grasp, "Yeah, I hear you."

"Nah, I told her that we were going to play cards over at Lamar's crib," B answers.

"Did she believe that bullshit?" I wonder taking a shot.

"I don't care if she did or didn't."

"Man you are stupid," I say shoving B in his arm.

"How often do we have someone in the family getting married? Shit, you are my boy! We are about to show out."

"Thanks man. Are you ready to go?" I say shaking his hand.

"Not before we kill this bottle G," B responds holding up the bottle.

B and I sit and sip slowly drinking up the bottle. Our phones are ringing off of the hook. We both are telling our callers that we will meet them at the club shortly.

We continue to reminisce and drink until the bottle is gone. B reminds me that I had Christian as my best-man, but now that he is gone, it is time for me to choose someone. Without any doubt in my mind, I choose him. Shit, B and I have been cool since we were kids.

B and I arrive at the strip club. The club parking-lot looks as if it's open for regular business. B says that Tone and himself told everyone I knew to come to celebrate with us. Knowing that it was time to put away my player's card everyone wanted to celebrate with me.

B and I walk in the club together, but to my surprise, there isn't any strippers dancing or on the poles. Keith greets us at the door with bottles in his hands.

"Are you ready for your big day homie?" Keith asks joyfully handing me a bottle.

"As ready as I am going to be," I respond.

"I hear you. This is a serious commitment," Keith adds.

"Exactly."

"Well, you don't have to worry about that until tomorrow," B interjects escorting me towards the fellas.

As we approach the large crowd of men, I notice a chair. This chair looks like a chair made for a king. It's gold with the red seat. A bucket of bills sit on the floor next to the chair.

"Have a seat," Keith orders.

"Oh, this is for me," I say surprised.

"Man, sit your ass down," B jokes.

Soon as I sit down, I hear a whistle blow. All of us look in the direction of the whistle sound. Three female waitresses enter with referee uniforms on and boy shorts. They walk around the club making sure that everyone's glass is full or they have whatever drinks they like. Some of the fellas flirt with the waitresses getting them to become a little loose.

"It's about to go down," B says blowing out a cloud of smoke from his blunt.

I search the room for any signs of what's to come. Everyone's eyes are searching as well as mine.

Suddenly, the lights dim. Smoke creeps across the stage like a scary movie. The DJ shouts at us to see if we are ready to have a good time. The hyped crowd shouts back then the lights completely go out. All that you can see is the exit signs near the doors and lights from the DJ booth. The strippers bust in with bright lights flashing them at all of us. Police sirens blasts through the speakers. The look on most of these hustlers' faces are nervous as hell. The strippers are dressed like cops. I sit excited rubbing my hands together. One of the stripper's strut towards me twirling her pair of handcuffs.

"Oh oh!" The DJ announces.

The stripper straddles me and begins to give me a lap dance. I allow her to twirk on top of me while I drink straight for the bottle. She whispers in my ear that she has a butt plug in her ass. I don't even know what that is, but I want to find out.

After a few minutes of grinding on me and staring in my eyes, she turns around showing me her fat apple. She bounces her ass like a Jamaican dance hall queen. She throws it in my lap and stands up so that I can get a clear visual. I have to admit that I like what I see. I take a fist full of money and douse her with cash.

I am truly enjoying myself. The fellas are too. Each stripper is putting on a show to keep all of our attention. Almost like clockwork, a fist full of money is being tossed in the air at the strippers every few minutes.

My stripper tears off her top revealing nothing but her breast. All of the other strippers follow suit. We all are amazed. More money is thrown.

Again she straddles me and purposely slaps me with her breast. The fellas are going nuts watching her tease me. She takes my hands and put them on her breast. I can feel that they are real. I caress her breasts and then begin to juggle them playfully. She laughs at my actions.

Skillfully, she takes my hand into her crotch. I can feel the heat from her pussy. With my hands put together, she sneaks and handcuffs me. She hops off of my lap and signal for her friends to come over.

Three strippers, including the main stripper who has been giving me all of the special attention, takes off my pants and shoes. They pull me on the stage and give everyone a show. I am now the center of attention.

Each girl takes their turn dry humping me. They all tease me with kisses and putting their mouth over my dick. I am freaking out. I am unable to touch or resist their touch. My dick is solid as a rock. Looks like I have a pop bottle sticking in my draws. They take body shots off of my chest and take turns pouring me shots. I am wasted.

The triple team climbs off and assists me back in my seat. I had to beg to get my pants back. I tip all of the girls very well for giving me a good time. The main girl gives me a kiss on the check and tells me to come visit her at the club any time. I tell her that I will take her up on her offer. I send her away with a hard slap on her ass. The fellas and I watch her ass shake as she walks away.

The strippers continue to work. They give personal dances and also kills the stage. These girls are so acrobatic. They are doing tricks on the poles with each other. The fellas go crazy like a pack of wild dogs every time two or more girls entertain another with some sexual shit. These girls are going all out.

B stubbles over to me spilling his drink, "Are you having a good time family?"

"Yeah man. I appreciate all of this. You really did your thing with this one."

"Man, anything for my real homies. The night is not over yet though," B says with a smile on his face. He turns his head away from me and nod at the stripper who was giving me the special attention.

I look at my watch noticing that it is way later than I expected. I wanted to be in the hotel room about two hours ago. I still had to do so much before the wedding.

"B, I have to get ready to head out!" I shout over the music.

"What? Why?" B shouts back screwing up his face.

"Man, I have to go. I have to get some rest before tomorrow," I respond standing up getting ready to leave out of the door.

"Reese, I don't think you will be getting any rest tonight," B says putting his arm around my shoulder.

We walk back to the stage and B tells the triple team to follow us to the hotel. I am shocked by his comments, but I don't reject the idea.

The ladies leave the stage and head for the dressing room. Minutes later, they come out with their bags and ready to go. The ladies talk amongst themselves.

"This is a wedding gift from Christian. I know that he would have done this for you," B slurs his words drunk as fuck.

"All of them?" I ask curiously.

"Yeah man. All of them," B answers slapping my hands happy for me.

The ladies circle around me. We walk throughout the club saying our goodbyes to everyone. The fellas already know what time it is. Before I walk out the door, I notice B damn near sleep that fast. I knew the liquor has caught up with him. I have to take him to the hotel and get him a room.

The ladies follow me to the hotel. B slept the whole way. He would occasionally blurt out something, but I couldn't understand his drunk ass.

I give the ladies a key to my room and ask them to meet me in the room. They all quickly rush for the elevator.

I pay for a room for B. The desk looks at us like some drunk fools, but the knot I pull out changes that look really fast.

Trying to hold him up down the hallway is hilarious. B keeps falling up against doors causing for folks to step out and check for what is going on. I just laugh at him.

Finally, I get him to his room. He thanks me for looking out for him. I remind him that I need him up early so that we can be ready before the wedding. He assures me that he will be up and ready by 8 in the morning. I shake his hand and head for the door. B stops me in my tracks and asks me to come back over to him. Standing in front of him, it's hard to laugh. He looks like an old drunk trying to keep his eyes open. B digs in his pockets and hands me a box of condoms.

Right on time.

I rush out of his room choosing to hit the stairs believing that the elevator will take longer. I hop up the stairs in no time.

The closer I get to my room, I can smell the familiar smell of loud. I mean this weed has the whole floor stinking good.

Opening the door, I am greeted with three naked women lounging around. One of the ladies gets up and brings me a blunt to smoke. I feel like a mob boss. She turns away to walk back to her seat, and I slap her ass just to say thanks.

I don't hesitate to strip down to my boxers. I take a few hits of the blunt and set it aside. I reach in my pockets and pull out the box of condoms. The stripper who has been giving me the most attention stands up and walks between my legs.

"What are you going to do with them?" She asks looking down at the box of condoms.

"Just in case something goes down," I answer.

"Do you want something to go down?" She questions licking her lips.

"Hell yeah!"

"Like what?"

"I will like to see if you can really fuck me or if that was just how you dance," I reply waiting for her response.

"Damn! I guess that was an honest answer. You are about to be a lucky man. China and Therapy, let's give him a good time."

The girls surround me. I give each of them a kiss and feel all over them. I don't know whose hands are stroking my shafts, but it feels like their playing tug of war with it. I put my head back and enjoy their tongues skillfully scrolling over my dick. I look down still unable to believe that I have three bad ass women sucking my dick at once. I wish I was recording this.

China stops sucking on my dick and starts to treat my balls. I grab the other girls head and watch them suck the hell out of my dick. I catch China playing with the main stripper's pussy. That shit turned me on even more. I finally find out her name when Therapy asks her to get the box of condoms. Her name is Sky.

Sky takes out a condom and rolls it down my dick. She licks my balls and gives me a hard jerk before getting up. She tells the other two girls to wait for us in the room while she handles her business. They slowly walk away watching Sky's next move.

Sky hops up on the couch standing over me. Her neatly shaved pussy is right in my face. She begins to sway and dip down rubbing against my penis. Although I have a condom on, I can feel her wetness as if I was bare. Sky bends over and licks my neck seductively. I place both of my hands on the top of her ass and try to push her down so that she could ride me, but she rejects the idea. She looks at me and smiles. Not knowing what to do next, I sit back and allow her to take control. She places her hands on my thighs and pushed herself up putting her feet against the wall. I don't know what to think, but this girl his wild; ass and pussy all in my face. She strokes my dick hardening it to her liking. While she is jacking me off, I spread her ass cheeks and work my tongue over her pussy getting it good and wet.

"Let me take this condom off," she asks.

I don't even think about what she said until I felt her pulling the condom off.

Sky sucks the tip of my dick and strokes me simultaneously. The feeling is driving me crazy. I try to compete with her and flick the tip of my tongue rapidly over her clit. Sky changes up her position just a little. She puts her elbows into my thighs and knees into my chest. Now I have a perfect angle to suck on her pussy better. I can feel her body shaking each time I lick her click, but she begins to throw her ass back. I start to tongue fuck her pussy and switch back to licking her click until I bust all in her mouth.

Sky slides down my body and tries to stick my dick in her but I refuse. There's no way I was going into any woman raw besides Diana.

"Give me a minute," I tell her for an excuse.

"Well, when you are ready, don't forget to come in here and give these ladies some of that good dick," Sky says walking into the bedroom.

I hurry to get up out of my seat. I reach down and grab the condoms.

Following right behind Sky, I am thinking about getting some of her pussy. Her ass jiggles with each step getting my dick back to form. I have already put in the work to get her ready now I have to work double duty.

Walking in, I notice that the other girls didn't waste a minute to go at it. Sky and I enter the bedroom and Therapy is tasting all of China's juices. China's moans assures me that Therapy is doing a good job. Therapy's little ass looks good. Both of them are skinny but have athletic bodies. China's body looks better than Therapy's. China has a fatter ass and bigger breasts. Therapy seems like she is more of the freak but they both can get it.

Therapy twirks her ass cheeks for my delight, so I go behind her and slap each cheek. She lifts her head up and let out a moan. When she lifts her head away from China's lap, I see that China has her clit pierced.

Damn these girls are some freaks!

Sky takes a seat in a love seat and directs me to follow right behind Therapy. China blows me a kiss. I stand at the side of the bed watching Therapy. I play with myself to keep it hard and ready. China reaches for my penis. She shoves it down her throat. While she is sucking me off, I notice Sky going to town playing with herself watching all of us. Sky has her leg propped up for a deep penetration.

After a few minutes of sucking my dick, China sits up and Therapy rolls over and lies on the bed. China shuffles across the bed towards me on her knees. With one hand, she holds my dick, and the other, she plays with herself.

"I want you to fuck the shit out of me!" China orders positioning herself in doggy-style.

"No bitch, he is going to fuck me!" Sky snaps climbing off of the sofa.

Sky lies back on the bed and puts her legs back. I study her sexy ass body while I slide on a condom. China catches an attitude but dives in to exchange the favor with Therapy.

I slap my dick on her pussy as a fair warning of what's to come. Sky licks her lips and squeezes her breasts becoming uncontrollably horny. I play with her and slide my dick in and take it back out a few times. Sky tries to hold me down with her legs, but I manage to get loose. Pushing her legs back, I tell her to hold her legs. I grab my manhood and thrust forcefully into her.

While I am banging the fuck out of Sky, China keeps looking over at me. I take my left hand and caress her ass. She takes it and put it between her legs. I am sliding my fingers in and out of her dripping wet pussy at the same speed that I am hitting Sky.

Although Sky's pussy is good as fuck, I wanted some of China's and China wanted some of me. Every time I look over at China, Sky works her hips to regain my attention. I slow down my rhythm, and I pull China off of Therapy. Sky is looking at me in disbelief. I whisper in China's ear that I want her.

China climbs on top of Sky and give her a passionate kiss. She sucks on her bottom lip. China slides down her body until she reaches Sky's sweet spot. I keep eye contact with Sky while China licks on her goodie spot. I get right behind China and slide it in. She don't hesitate to throw it back on me. I challenge her and hit her harder when she comes back to me. My force is causing Sky's breast to bounce around. The three of us are having a great time, but Therapy sits on the edge of the bed just watching. I signal for her to join in and Sky catches my gesture. Sky tells Therapy to give her a kiss and they go at it. Before I knew it, Sky was eating Therapy and I was deep into some wet pussy. Therapy is crouched over Sky's face holding onto the headboard and Sky is enjoying the whole moment.

We all finish having multiple orgasms. We all lay in the bed drinking and smoking talking about the night. China and Therapy fall asleep first. Sky is right up under me telling me that she would like to be my side chick. It's very tempting, but I tell her that after tomorrow, I was going to be a new man. She looks at me like I am full of shit. She quickly reminds me what she is capable of and all she wanted was a man to take care of her. I told her that we will remain friends, but I wasn't in a rush to fuck up my marriage before it even started. She accepts my friendship, but I know in the back of her mind she believes that she could get the dick at anytime.

CHAPTER 12

REESE

I am awakened by the sound of a door closing. I look around the room and Sky isn't in sight. The other two girls are on my left knocked out. I know she wouldn't leave her friends hear alone. Maybe she went for coffee. Damn, I would've order room service.

Sky suddenly walks back in, in a hurry. Her breasts are bouncing rapidly with each step. I am wondering where did she go not wearing any clothes but here comes in the fellas including my barber.

"Aw shit," Lamar says looking in my bed.

"I see somebody had a little too much fun last night," Tone joke lifting the sheet looking at the other two women.

"Are you sure you are ready to do this?" B questions seating in the loveseat.

"Hell yeah! What time is it?" I respond sitting up in the bed. I search the room with my eyes looking for the hotel clock, but I guess we lost that in the middle of an epic night.

B, checks his watch, "It's almost ten."

"Shit, I have to be at the church by 12:00 a.m."

"We are ready!" Tone opens his mouth to say.

"Ladies can y'all excuse me. I have to get my shit together."

"So you are going to kick us out?" Sky asks frowning.

"No. I just need to get dressed," I answer.

"Hell yeah he's kicking y'all out. You ain't his woman! Here is a couple dollars for your troubles," Tone interjects.

"Boy, I don't want your money," Sky says walking into the bathroom.

The ladies leave after getting dressed. I didn't have a chance to say goodbye or even excuse my friend's manners because time is of the essence.

The barber starts on my head and the fellas all want to hear what went down. I give them a little bit of the story, but I kept a few things to myself. They don't need to know all of my business. They pretty much know what went down when you enter a room full of naked women.

While they all are getting their fresh cuts, I finish getting dressed. I put on my watch and notice that we only have thirty minutes to get to the wedding.

I rush into the living room, "Ay, let's go. If I ain't there on time, Diana will kill me."

"No, she will kill you if she knew you were in here making pornos," Tone jokes.

B hopes in with me in my car and the fellas follow behind us. B and I talk about the day I first met Diana. He was right there.

Diana was with her friends in the mall doing some shopping. I didn't have the courage to talk to her, but I wanted her to know I was watching. I followed her around until she stopped and came to me. As nervous as I was to speak, I was glad that I didn't have to. She had her number written on a piece of paper and asked me to call her later.

B and I just gotten in the game and all we did was shop. We didn't know the meaning of stacking money then. Our main focus was getting paid and shopping. We wanted to have the flashy jewels, designer clothes, and ride on some Dayton's. In our hood, all the girls loved us but Diana was different. I had to have her.

Soon as we pull up in front of the museum, people are rushing me to get inside. Diana's sister comes out and is cussing me out, but I deserve every word. She turns her mouth off as soon as we walk inside putting on a fake smile.

The fellas and I speed walk down the aisle and the music begins to play. My aunt asks where have I been, but I just laugh. The fellas laugh also. She doesn't find anything funny.

Rico walks behind the flower girl looking like a little me in his suit. He is carefully walking slowly so that he doesn't drop the rings.

I look over my shoulder wishing my brother was standing next to me. I know that he is smiling down on us.

B shakes my hand, "Proud of you man. For real."

"I am ready for it," I say hugging him.

Surprise to see a national recording artists start walking down the aisle singing our wedding song. He is wearing a matching tuxedo like the rest of the wedding party. I look over at the wedding planner who stands near the entrance. She waves at me smiling. *More money*, I think to myself.

The artist stands with the pastor continuing to sing. Diana enters looking like she'd just walked out of a dream. We stare at each other before she starts to walk. Her and her father's brother walks down the aisle together. Diana waves at some friends and family members.

"Mommy you are pretty!" Rico blurts out. Everyone laughs.

I start to reminisce on all of the good and bad times we had that lead us up to this moment. I drug her through the mud. She took all of my late nights, running the streets, my prison stench, arguments, and cheating ways. Most importantly she was by my side when my brother died. Diana truly loved me and only wanted me to make this dream a reality for her.

Tears of joy begin to drop from my face watching how happy my baby is. The ladies in the crowd notice and all announce how sweet it is. My aunt even starts crying, and she didn't even cry at my mother's funeral.

Wiping my eyes, I hear my boys laughing at me, but I don't care about their jokes. I am marrying the woman of my dreams. Diana is taking me for me with all of the shit I bring. I am happy to become her husband.

Diana and I have our eyes locked on each other while the pastor speaks. I don't hear a word that he is saying because I am so focused on her. I do notice her uncle letting go of her arm. She carefully steps in front of me. We hold hands and listen to the pastor speak from the Bible.

The pastor tells our guests that we have written our own vows and would like to share them. Diana goes first. I am as still as concrete while she shares with everyone the reason why she loves me. I can't help but to tear up again. When Diana finishes, I read mine. Diana cries also.

Diana, I promise to love and care for you until the end of time. I promise that I will love you as my friend and partner. I promise to talk to you and also listen. I promise to trust and appreciate you. I promise to share my dreams with you as we continue to turn those dreams into reality.

I will join my life with yours and together we will face all of life has to offer. I will be the best man that I can be. I will protect you and your heart.

I promise to be honest with you, respect you, and cherish you for as long as we both shall live.

Baby you mean everything to me. You have been there for me when I didn't have much and you continued to weather the storm when times became better. Making you happy means the world to me. And for the rest of our life I want to continue to do so.

Everyone is feeling my words. The guests all clap like we had touched each one of them with our words. I look around the room and a lot of people are in tears.

Diana leans in to kiss me but the pastor intervenes.

"Wait a minute now. We will get to that part in a second," the pastor jokes.

The crowd laughs.

"Diana Jane Harris would you take Maurice White to be your husband?"

"I do," Diana Responds.

I place the princess cut ring on her finger.

"Maurice White would you take Diana Jane Harris to be your wife. To have and to hold and cherish forever?"

"I…"

I am cut off by a stamped of cops and alphabet boys.

"Everyone stay where you are! This is the DEA! We have arrest warrants for Maurice White and other members of the so called 75 boys!" Agent Tony Rivera shouts walking in behind the army of cops.

"Reese!" Diana cries.

"Baby, call my lawyer."

"I will," Diana reply.

Lamar rushes for the back to escape. Four cops run off after him. The rest of us just stand here waiting to hear why we are being arrested.

"Reese, I told you I will have my chance to see you again. You should have worked with me," Agent Rivera provokes.

"What are you here doing man? I ain't doing anything," I respond.

"You are arrested for the distribution of narcotics in the state of Ohio," he answers.

"You got the wrong guy."

"Yeah okay. Agent Jackson please come and tell me if we have the wrong man," Agent Tony says sarcastically.

"Who the fuck is Agent Jackson?" I ask.

Candace.

"We got him," Agent Rivera announces.

Candace walks up on me and nods her head at Agent Rivera, "Yes we do."

Candace forcefully turns me around and puts on a pair of handcuffs. I am laughing at the thought of her being a cop. When she turns me around, I am staring at her badge on her neck chain. This bitch can't be a DEA agent.

I watch other agents take my boys out of the museum one by one. The three of them are already in police cars when I come out. Candace and Agent Tony Rivera pull me out to an unmarked car.

Diana screams, "Baby, the lawyer is on his way downtown now."

"You got you a good one, huh? If she only knew that she won't be jumping the broom with you for a while. I hope she keeps that cute dress for a better man," Candace adds.

"You should've stayed out of the dope game Reese. Now we got your ass!" Agent Rivera says pushing me in the back of the car.

****

A month of lying on this hard ass bunk has my back all fucked up. I have complained but these doctors don't care. I just can't wait to get some good news from my lawyer today. He passed the tape I had of Candace and myself having sex along to her boss and prosecutor. I pray that the tape help me, but I know it will hurt my relationship with Diana.

Diana has been down here to see me every other day. She is always in good spirits and hoping for the best. Diana believes that I will beat this case, but I am not too sure.

"White, you have a lawyer visit," the deputy shouts unlocking the cell door.

I am escorted to a separate room by a deputy. He makes me walk in front of him with my shoulder close to the wall. It was a rule not to cross over the yellow line in the hallways.

Sitting in the room with my head against the cold steel table, I am excited and nervous at the same time. Diana already told me that the lawyer has found some leaks in my case, but I want to hear it from his mouth.

My lawyer comes in with a pack of papers. It is my "discovery packet." Reading the packet, it's talking about some old shit;

when I used to put people on in the city with my crew - most of it is talking about Christian. The packet tells the date and time that we hooked up in front of the Laundromat. I knew they got that information from Candace. What surprise me at the end of the packet is pictures of the crew and myself at the club, at Keith's, with Big Mike, and finally pictures of the crew doing deals. I continue to read and turn pages till I get to a page with Detective Shaw and myself meeting at the gas station.

The lawyer tells me that Detective Shaw found out that we set him and he returned the favor with feds. I sit wondering all of the information he could have on us.

Detective Shaw told the feds that I was the main dealer from the crew. They were after me the hardest because they like taking down the leader and trying to flip him. I wasn't going for it. J and his team of killas would have us killed in a heartbeat.

It's crazy how people get paid and freed from prison to snitch on someone else. My lawyer warns me that Shaw is off limits. Trying to get to Shaw will make the case easy for the prosecutor plus add more time to any sentence I receive. Shaw is in protective custody somewhere until trial.

I remind my lawyer that they don't have much on me but word of mouth. Candace can only testify that she seen me get a package from Christian but she couldn't confirm what was in it.

I have this case beat, I said to myself.

"Reese, I want to tell you that you have bigger problems than Shaw," The lawyer says.

"What's worse than this shit?" I ask pounding my fist against the table. I stand up to listen to his next words.

The lawyer grabs his stuff rapidly, "I just found out this morning that one of your co-defendants is testifying against you."

"What! Aw, hell nah!" I shout not believing him.

"He also wore a wire on you. I will get all of that evidence shortly."

"What the fuck! Who is it?" I rush over to my lawyer and snatch his ass up grabbing his tie.

"Help me! Deputy! Help!" He screams at the top of his lungs.

I pick him up off of his feet. I stare him dead in his eyes letting him know that I can kill him right now.

"Motherfucka, I am paying you too much fucking money not to be giving me answers!"

The deputy fumbles with the keys and shouts for another guard to buzz the door open.

"Please Mr. White put me down," the lawyer pleads swinging his feet.

"White, get down on the floor! I will mace your ass! A deputy shoots.

I continue to shout threats at my lawyer until a gang of deputies knock me down to the floor. I am maced in my eyes and shocked. Not giving them the reaction they want from being shocked, they hit me again. I am on the floor shouting threats at them until I feel them tying my hands together. They carry me back to an empty cell and let me suffer in pain. Minutes later, when I calm down, a nurse enters the room with a deputy and checks me out.

After cleaning my eyes out, I sit and think about what the lawyer said. All of the pictures play in my mind. Who would tell on me? What are they getting out of it? Who got caught up before all of this shit hit the fan? So many questions I had asked myself.

With my face in my hands, I think of all of my friends and think of who could it be. No one's names are popping into my head. I am becoming frustrated with the thought of someone that I have known for many years to turn on me.

No one respected the rules of the game anymore; too many snitches and greedy muthafuckas. Players change but the game stays the same. There will be another hustler taking over the streets with the idea of becoming rich and getting out of their situation.

The game ain't over!

www.ingramcontent.com/pod-product-compliance
Lightning Source LLC
Chambersburg PA
CBHW060038040426
42331CB00032B/1015